0254741

D1756372

Long Loan

This book is due for return on or before the last date shown below

0 3 JAN 2007		
0 4 FEB 2008		

St Martins Services Ltd

Adam Publishers & Distributors
New Delhi -2 (India)

ADAM PUBLISHERS & DISTRIBUTORS

Exporters & Importers
1542, Pataudi House, Darya Ganj
New Delhi-110002
Phone (O) : 23282550, 23284740
Tele/Fax:23267510 (R) 95120-2413957
e-mail : apd@bol.net.in
        apdbooks@yahoo.co.in
www.adambooks.com

Edition - 2004
ISBN : 81-7435-040-3

Printed & Bound in India
Published by :
Syed Sajid Ali
ADAM PUBLISHERS & DISTRIBUTORS

1542, Pataudi House, Darya Ganj
New Delhi-110002

Contents

PREFACE

Belief in the Angels is one of the pillars of Islam. Allah Almighty says:

$$\text{امَنَ الرَّسُولُ بِمَا أُنْزِلَ إِلَيْهِ مِنْ رَّبِّهِ وَ الْمُؤْمِنُونَ}$$

$$\text{كُلٌّ امَنَ بِاللهِ وَمَلَآئِكَتِهِ وَكُتُبِهِ وَرُسُلِهِ}$$

"The Messenger believeth in what hath been revealed to him from his Lord, as do the men of faith, each one (of them) believeth in Allah, His Angels, His Books and His Messengers." (Q. 2:285).

These Angels were created from light. They have their own world of lights and have nothing to do but to keep glorifying Allah Almighty and carry out His orders in each sphere of His creation and He has Himself praised for such a delicate creation,. The Holy Qur'an says:

$$\text{الْحَمْدُ لِلّٰهِ فَاطِرِ السَّمٰوٰتِ وَالْأَرْضِ جَاعِلِ الْمَلَآئِكَةِ رُسُلًا}$$

$$\text{أُولِى أَجْنِحَةٍ مَثْنٰى وَثُلَاثَ وَرُبَاعَ يَزِيدُ فِى الْخَلْقِ مَا يَشَآءُ إِنَّ اللهَ}$$

$$\text{عَلٰى كُلِّ شَىْءٍ قَدِيْرٌ}$$

"Praise be to Allah, the Originator of the heavens and the earth, Who made the Angels messengers with wings--two, or three, or four (pairs). He adds to Creation as He pleases : for Allah has power over all things". (Q. 35:1).

That is they are messengers or instruments of Allah's Will, and may have few or numerous Errands entrusted to them. Allah Almighty says:

$$\text{لَيْسَ الْبِرَّ أَنْ تُوَلُّوا وُجُوهَكُمْ قِبَلَ الْمَشْرِقِ وَ}$$

$$\text{فَأَصْلِحُوا بَيْنَهُمْ فَلَا إِثْمَ عَلَيْهِ إِنَّ اللهَ غَفُورٌ رَّحِيْمٌ يَآأَيُّهَا}$$

$$\text{كُتِبَ عَلَى الَّذِيْنَ}$$

"It is not righteousnes that ye turn your faces towards East or West; but it is righteousness--to believe in Allah and the

Last Day , and the Angels, and the Book, and the Messengers......" (Q. 2:177)

The first requirement of true piety is the right belief in Allah, and the Last Day, and the Angels, and the Books, and His Prophets. The order of the different articles of belief is very significant. Belief in Allah implies that one should also believe that Allah has not created human beings as mere playthings, but He has created them as responsible beings who are held accountable to Him for all their deeds and misdeeds. Then it is through His Angels that His commands are executed and the revelations are delivered to the Prophets. These revelations contain the Will of Allah and are the unerring guide to humanity.

Allah Almighty has therefore said:

وَمَنْ يَّكُفُرْ بِاللّٰهِ وَمَلْٰٓبِكَتِهِ وَكُتُبِهِ وَرُسُلِهِ اللّٰهَ اِلَّا قَلِيْلًا ۞ مُّنَ نُبُنْبِيْنَ بَيْنَ بَعِيْدًا

"Any who denieth Allah, His Angels, His Books, His Messengers, and the Day of Judgement, hath gone far astray." (Q. 4:136).

That is if your belief is by habit or birth or the example of those you love or respect or admire, make that belief more specific and personal to yourself. We must not only have faith, but realise that faith in our inmost being. The chief objects of your Faith are Allah, His Messengers, and His Revelations. To all these we must give a home in our hearts. The Angels we do not see and realise as we realise Allah, who is nearer to us than our jugular vein.

These and many other *ayahs* make it clear without an iota of doubt that belief in the angels is a basic tenet of belief. If a person, therefore, denies the existence of the angels, he also denies the revelation of the Divine Books. That is why the Qur'an mentions belief in the Angels before belief in the Divine Books and the

Messengers.

M/s Adam Publishers and Distributors have made it a point to publish a series of books on the fundamentals of Islam to educate the Muslims and non-Muslims alike.

May Allah Almighty grace our efforts with success.

Badr Azimabadi
Jamia Nagar, Okhla
10 - 1- 1996
NEW DELHI- 110025

Angels

The guidance of man through revelation is one of the most important manifestations of the Mercy of Allah Who has been revealing His Will to the humanity through the succession of the Prophets, the last being Mohammed (peace and blessings of Allah be upon him) through whom the Holy Qur'an was vouchsafed to the humanity. The Qur'an testifies and affirms what the earlier Books had said. The Qur'an was revealed not to startle the world with unheard of novelties but to carry the moral and religious development of mankind to new stages, transcending and yet fulfilling the previous stages, continuous with them and finalising them.

Allah Almighty says:

وَإِذْ قَالَ رَبُّكَ لِلْمَلَٰئِكَةِ إِنِّى جَاعِلٌ فِى الْأَرْضِ خَلِيفَةً قَالُوٓا۟ أَتَجْعَلُ فِيهَا مَن يُفْسِدُ فِيهَا وَيَسْفِكُ الدِّمَآءَ وَنَحْنُ نُسَبِّحُ بِحَمْدِكَ وَنُقَدِّسُ لَكَ قَالَ إِنِّىٓ أَعْلَمُ مَا لَا تَعْلَمُونَ ۝

"Behold, thy Lord said to the Angels; "I will create a vicegerent on earth". They said: "Will Thou place therein one who will make mischief therein and shed blood?--Whilst we do celebrate Thy praises and glorify Thy Holy (name)?" He said: "I know what Ye know not". (Q. 2:30).

It would seem that the Angels, though holy and pure, and endued with power from Allah, yet represented only one side of Creation. We may imagine them without passion or emotion, of which the highest flower is love. If man was to be endued with emotions, those emotions could lead him to the highest and drag him to the lowest. The power of will or choosing would have to go with them, in order that man might steer his own bark. This power of will (when used aright) gave him to some extent mastery over his own fortunes and over nature, thus bringing him nearer to God-like nature, which has supreme mastery and will. We may suppose the angels had no independent wills of thier own : their perfection in other ways reflected Allah's perfection but could not raise them to the dignity of vicegereny. The perfect vicegerent is he who has the power of initiative himself, but whose independent action always reflects perfectly the will of his Principal. The angels in their one-sidedness saw only the mischief consequent on the misuse of the emotional nature by man; perhaps they also, being without emotions, did not understand the whole of Allah's nature, which gives and asks of love. In humility and true devotion to Allah, they remonstrate : we must not imagine the least tinge of jealousy, as they are without emotion. This mystery of love being above them, they are told that they do not know, and they acknowledge not their fault (for there is no question of fault) but their imperfection of knowledge. At the same time, the matter is brought home to them when the actual capacities of man are shown to them.

What we learn from the Qur'an is that Adam was a new entrant in the universe who had a new role to play and he was, therefore, endowed with some distinctive qualities which the other species lacked and his most distinguishing quality is that he has been made a trustee of a free personality to fulfill the designs of Allah on the earth. The angels apprehended that since Adam had been fashioned out of clay, he would, therefore, misuse the authority Allah had delegated to him. He would thus spread corrruption and shed blood. The angels were at a loss to know the necessity of the creation of Adam, when they in countless numbers were already there, ready to carry out the commands of Allah Almighty.

Allah, the Creator of the universe, had before Him a special purpose for the fulfillment of which He was going to create Adam. The idea behind it was to manifest that the material world is not profane and the natural urges of man are not ignoble as man is primarily a spiritual being inspite of the fact that it is material body in which man's soul is treasured. Thus man would no doubt commit evil because of lapses on his part but would not absolutely succumb to low desires, he would rather live upto the hgh ideals as the true servant of Allah Almighty, even though he has been given freedom to commit evil, if he so desires. The man would, therefore, not only elevate his material life to the spiritual height, and prove that there is nothing profane in the world, but would also show by his deeds that he is the faithful servant of the Lord, though he is free to act otherwise. The apprehension of the Angels that man would always spread corruption and shed blood has been proved to be baseless. Man has always been striving for the better, for the peace and prosperity and delivering the goods and it is on basis of these positive virtues and urge for constructive work that mankind has been able to create a social order. There could have been no ideas of corporate life, if man had been corrupt by his very nature, always ready to act treacherously. That a man leads a social life is an undeniable proof of the fact that the good in man significantly predominates the evil in man. He, at times, without doubt yields to low desires and behaves like a brute, but it is not his real nature, it is a lapse on his part and there is always a yearning in him to revert to the original good in him.

It should be remembered that it is too much to expect infallibility from the man, as he has been made of the stuff which can he tempted to commit evil, but his noble self, however, which is in fact his real self, revolts against evil. There are occasions when he fails to resist these temptations and falls in their snares, but he feels remorseful and strengthens his ego in order to safeguard himself against this mishap on another occasion. Unless the man is completely devoid of moral sense, there is a strong urge in him to fight against evil and promote good. Man cannot banish evil altogether and behave like an Angel, but he is primarily a champion of good and a fighter against evil, and it is with this nature that he has been created by Allah Almighty. He, therefore, falls in a distinctive category in Allah's scheme of creations--distinctive from lifeless matter; from the Angels, and from Jinn and his role is different from all these categories, --which if put briefly may be stated,-- his is the role of vicegerent of Allah upon the earth, being the trustee of the free persoanlity. The Prophet of Allah (peace and blessings of Allah be upon him) has very beautifully explained the distinguishing feature of the specie called man. It is reported that Hazrat Abu Ayyub Ansari (may Allah be pleased with him) said at the time of his death: "I concealed from you something I heard from Allah's Messenger (peace and blessings of Allah be upon him) but now (when I am going to leave this world) I tell you that I heard him (the Holy Prophet) say : If you were not to commit faults, Allah would have created another creation, which would commit faults (and beg forgiveness) and He would forgive (that) ("Kitab-ut-Tauba", *Sahih Muslim*).

What this implies is that the distinguishing characteristic of man is that he is given freedom to do or not to do an act, but despite his freedom he behaves as a God-fearing person and whenever he commits faults, he turns to Allah Almighty in repentance and thus regains his spiritual and moral height. This submision to Allah's commands, and close and intimate contact with Him amidst irresistable temptations, is the distinctive feature of man which entitles him to be 'the crown of creation'.

It should also be remembered that *Khalifa* is one who exercises delegated powers on behalf of a supreme authority. Man, thus, is not the master but only His deputy and does not possess power of his own, except those only which are delegated to him by the real master.

It was not by way of any objection that the Angels uttered these words, but to seek information as to what necessity had arisen that man was being created upon the earth. If it were for carrying out at the behest of the Lord, the Angels were doing this work all right and if it were for the glorification of Allah it was also being done quite adequately by them. Thus apparently the Angels could not see any reason for the creation of human race. The Angels were tempted to put this question to the Lord fearing that there might have been some slackness on their part for which Allah Almighty had decided to bring into being a new creation.

So far as the Arabic words *tasbih* and *taqdis* are concerned, the former implies 'to submit oneself with perfect humiliation'. It can find expression both in language and behaviour. As regards language it implies to "sanctify" and as regards behaviour it means to submit to the commands of the Master cheerfully. *Taqdis* means to consecrate Allah and to hold Him pure from all conceivable failings and weaknesses which the people generally attribute to deities other than Allah Almighty.

Our knowledge is not so comprehensive as to fully comprehend the purpose for which Adam was being created. He was brought into existence not for any failing on the part of Angels but to play a specific role on the earth as the vicegerent of Lord.

Adam was the first progenitor of human race. He was a Prophet. After his departure from Paradise he was made to settle at a place between Tigris and Euphrates which is now-a-days called Iraq. He was named Adam, after the name of the surface of the earth or ground, as he had been fashioned out of clay. Some of the scholars are of the opinion that the progenitor of mankind was called Adam because of some redness of his skin.

The Holy Qur'an says :

وَعَلَّمَ اٰدَمَ الْاَسْمَآءَ كُلَّهَا ثُمَّ عَرَضَهُمْ عَلَى الْمَلٰٓئِكَةِ فَقَالَ
اَنْۢبِـُٔوْنِيْ بِاَسْمَآءِ هٰٓؤُلَآءِ اِنْ كُنْتُمْ صٰدِقِيْنَ

"And He taught Adam the names of all things; then He placed them before the Angels, and said : "Tell Me the names of these if ye are right."

قَالُواْ سُبْحَانَكَ لَاعِلْمَ لَنَآ إِلَّا مَا عَلَّمْتَنَآ إِنَّكَ أَنتَ الْعَلِيمُ الْحَكِيمُ ۞

"They said : "Glory to Thee : the knowledge we have none, save what Thou hast tought us : in truth it is Thou Who ist perfect in knowledge and wisdom."

قَالَ يَادَمُ أَنْبِئْهُم بِأَسْمَآئِهِمْ فَلَمَّا أَنبَأَهُم بِأَسْمَآئِهِمْ

"He said, "O Adam tell them their names". When he had told them their names, Allah said : "Did I not tell you that I know the secrets of heaven and earth, and I know what ye reveal and what you conceal ?"   (Q. 2:31-33).

"The names of things" according to commentators means the inner nature and qualities of things, and things here would include feelings. The particular qualities or feelings which were outside the nature of Angels were put by Allah into the nature of man. Man was thus able to love and understand love, and thus plan and initiate, as becomes office of vicegerent. The Angels acknowledged this. These things they could only know from the outside, but they have faith or belief in the Unseen. And they knew that Allah saw--what others see, what others do not see, what others may even wish to conceal. Man has many qualities which are latent or which he may wish to suppress or conceal, to his own deteriment.

It is through names that the human mind percieves things. The term *ism* (name) implies an expression 'conveying the knowledge' (of a thing) applied to denote a substance or an attirbute, for the purpose of distinction : in philisophical terminology it is a 'concept'. It is on the basic of this *ayah* that human being is held to be superior to the Angels. Allah Almighty taught Adam the names of all things and their respective attributes as without a clear knowledge of these Adam and his progeny could not be able to make proper use of them and acquit creditably of the responsiblity thrown upon them as the vicegerent of the Lord upon the earth.

The pronoun *hum* (these) shows that the subjects referred to here are not inanimate things, it is in subordination to the rational being. This provides a clear proof of the fact that not only names were presented to Adam, but a vision of rational beings animate or inanimate things was shown to Adam which were to become the manifestations of Allah's glory on earth.

Allah Almighty asked the Angels : `If your are right in your claim that you are competent to do everything and there is no necessity of the creation of Adam. 'In these words of Allah, the Angels could find reply to their query in regard to the creation of Adam that he would shed blood and spread corruption. Allah made it clear at the outset that He was not only going to confer upon Adam a limited autonomy but also endow him with knowledge enabling him to play the role of vicegerent of the Lord in a befitting manner.

When the Angels said:

قَالُوْا سُبْحٰنَكَ لَاعِلْمَ لَنَآ إِلَّا مَا عَلَّمْتَنَا إِنَّكَ أَنْتَ الْعَلِيْمُ الْحَكِيْمُ

"Glory be to Thee............." (2:32).

The expression is used to convey the idea that far above Thou art from doing anything which has any fault in it. The fault lies with us as our limited vision and limited knowledge fail to see and comprehend the good which lies in every aspect and phase of the Divine Plan.

And when the Angels said:

لَاعِلْمَ لَنَآ إِلَّا مَا عَلَّمْتَنَا

"We have no knowledge but what Thou hast taught us."
(2:32).

This is a death blow to the doctrine of Angelolatry. Angels are not all-knowing, but possess only that amount of knowledge which is given to them by Allah.

When Allah Almighty said:

قَالَ يَادَمُ أَنْبِئْهُمْ بِأَسْمَآئِهِمْ فَلَمَّآ أَنْبَأَهُمْ بِأَسْمَآئِهِمْ قَالَ أَلَمْ أَقُلْ لَكُمْ إِنِّى أَعْلَمُ غَيْبَ السَّمٰوٰتِ وَالْأَرْضِ وَأَعْلَمُ مَا تُبْدُونَ وَمَا كُنْتُمْ تَكْتُمُونَ ۝

"O Adam, inform them (angels) the names of those (objects). Then when he (Adam) had informed them the names of those He (Allah) said : ` Didn't I tell you 'verily I know the unseen in the heavens and earth and know what you disclose, and what you conceal."   (Q. 2:33).

According to some commentators Allah Almighty had not only enumerated the names of objects but also their attributes and characteristics and their intrinsic values. And hence Allah Almighty bestowed many excellences vicegerency and caliphate on Adam because of his wonderful knowledge of objects and matters. Such a knowledge is all the more necessary for worldly power, material gain and spiritual height. Knowledge is no less important for a ruler and a man in power. Hence knowledge of man and material is but essential for all human excellences and Allah Almighty has offered His exclusive blessings for men striving for acquiring knowledge. Some *ayahs* may be quoted below to highlight the importance of knowledge:

يَرْفَعِ اللّٰهُ الَّذِينَ اٰمَنُوا مِنْكُمْ وَالَّذِينَ أُوتُوا الْعِلْمَ دَرَجٰتٍ وَاللّٰهُ بِمَا تَعْمَلُونَ خَبِيرٌ ۝

"Allah will raise to high ranks those that have faith and knowledge among you. He is cognizant of all your actions."
(Q. 58:11).

مَلْ يَسْتَوِى الَّذِينَ يَعْلَمُونَ وَالَّذِينَ لَايَعْلَمُونَ إِنَّمَا يَتَذَكَّرُ اُولُوا الْأَلْبَابِ ۞

"Are those equal, those who know and those who do not know?" It is those who are endued with understanding that receive admonition."
(Q. 39:9).

لَا اِلَهَ اِلَّا هُوَ وَالْمَلَئِكَةُ وَاُولُوا الْعِلْمِ قَائِمًا بِالْقِسْطِ شَهِدَاللهُ اَنَّهُ لَا اِلَهَ اِلَّا هُوَالْعَزِيزُالْحَكِيمُ

"Allah bears witness and so do the Angels and those endued with knowledge that there is no god but He, the Maintainer of equity; there is no god but He, the Mighty, the Wise."
(Q. 3:18).

In the above *ayah* Allah bears witness' through His revelations and through the nature of His creation' that it has been brought into being by a consciously Planning Power and with a moral purpose behind it.

The basic fact that there is no god but Allah has been meaningfully repeated twice in this *ayah* in two different contexts. One is that since He alone is the Lord and Object of worship it is upon Him that lies the responsibility of maintaining equity in the universe. Secondly, since He is the Mightiest of the Mighty, He alone therefore manages to do it. Allah, the Real Sovereign of the universe is also the maintainer of Equity. This equity is to be observed both in the physical realm and the moral sphere of life. It is because of this equity that we find all the physical phenomena working according to a set plan of the Mighty Planner. There is not the least deviation from it and had it not been so the universe would have been smashed to pieces.

The same equity is to be mentioned in the social and moral life of man and it is for the observance of this equity in this sphere of man's life that Allah has given a Divine Code of life, al-Islam, which means complete surrender of man to the Will of Allah. Just as any deviation in the physical sphere gives rise to the severe destruction in the same way any deviation from Islam disturbs the equity and the poise between individual and society and results in moral and social chaos in the humanity. So long as the groups and people observe this equity they are able to live in peace and harmony and their development is harmonious, but as soon as they abandon this Right Path, and equity is distrubed, they are driven to ruin and devastation, and are ultimately swept out of effective existence in the world giving place to those whose thought and deeds conform to the Law of Equity as expressed and enunciated in Islam. Surrendering of one's self to the Will of the Lord is essential as it is by this attitude and behaviour alone that the equity is maintained in the moral, spiritual and social life of humanity, but if a man does not live up to this ideal, he meets destruction in this world and receives punishment in the life Hereafter as Merciful Lord cannot tolerate an attitude of man by which the equity is disturbed.

Allah Almighty determines the main role of His Messenger (peace and blessings of Allah be upon him) in the following *ayah*:

لَقَدْ مَنَّ اللّٰهُ عَلَى الْمُؤْمِنِيْنَ اِذْ بَعَثَ فِيْهِمْ رَسُوْلًا
اَوَكَانُوْا غُرًّى لَوْكَانُوْا عِنْدَ نَامَا مَاتُوْا وَمَا قَتَلُوْا لِيَجْعَلَ
وَالْحِكْمَةَ وَاِنْ كَانُوْا مِنْ قَبْلُ لَفِيْ ضَلٰلٍ مُّبِيْنٍ

"Indeed Allah has conferred a great favour upon the believers when He raised up in their midst an apostle from themselves, who recites to them His *ayahs*, and

purifies them, and teaches them the Book and Wisdom--
whereas afore they were surely in error manifest "
(Q. 3:164).

That is, a Prophet in Islam is not a mere medium, an inert,
mechanical transmitter of Divine truths, but a teacher, interpreter,
purifier of human hearts and expounder of profound truths revealed
to Him in the light of the Divine Wisdom given to him by Allah. He
is a repository of virtue, honesty and integrity and is most eminently
fit to convey the Divine Message to the people perfectly in
accordance with the Command of Allah, and to explain and
expound that with the Divine Wisdom conferred upon him. It is thus
the greatest favour of Allah upon mankind that a Prophet has been
raised from amongst human beings who has brought them out from
the darkness of ignorance into the light of Divine Faith.

Following this Allah Almighty says:

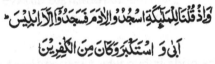

"And when we said to the Angels: Prostrate yourselves
before Adam, they prostrated themselves except *Iblis*. He
refused and waxed proud and became (one) of the
unbelivers." **(Q. 2:34).**

That is, not only Angels but all other beings lower than Angels
were meant to prostrate before Adam. Here the Angels have been
particularly brought into prominence because they occupy a higher
rank than Jinns. Thus the pronoun `fasajadu' covers both the
Angels and the Jinn. Prostration is symbolic of submission of
everything in the universe before man. The Angels and other beings
might have actually fallen into prostration to him as they were
commanded by Allah.

The literal meaning of *Iblis* is 'desperate', 'having been deprived' from the root-verb *ablasa*, the despaired or gave up hope or broken in spirit. It is the name given to a jinn who disobeyed Allah and refused to bow down before Adam as a symbol of his submission to him and his progeny and begged the Lord to grant him opportunity of seducing mankind to evil upto the Last Day. He is called Satan. He is not merely an abstract power of evil, but a being having a personality of his own. He was not an angel, but one amongst the jinns, who form a species of their own like Angels. The fact that *Iblis* was not an Angel but one amongst the jinns is testified by the Qur'an:

وَإِذْ قُلْنَا لِلْمَلَٰٓئِكَةِ اسْجُدُوا لِلْأَدَمَ فَسَجَدُوٓا إِلَّا إِبْلِيسَ كَانَ مِنَ الْجِنِّ فَفَسَقَ عَنْ أَمْرِ رَبِّهِۦ

"And (remember) when We said unto the Angels : Prostrate before Adam, and they fell prostrate, all save *Iblis*. He was of the jinn and he broke the Command of his Lord"

(Q. 18:50).

It was the pride in him which incited *Iblis* to disobey the command of Allah Alimghty. He was actuated to do so as he thought himself to be superior to Adam since he was made of fire whereas Adam had been fashioned out of clay. This pride and haughtiness was not ingrained in the very nature of *Iblis*, but he developed it out of his own will.

Allah's Messenger (peace and blessings of Allah be upon him) is reported to have said:

"Surely Satan has certain signs in his relationship with him, and surely the Angels have a certain sign in their relationship with men. The sign of Satan is to whisper that which is bad and to disbelieve in the Truth. The sign of the angels is to whisper that which is good and to believe in the Truth, so whoever amongst you finds these things which are good let him know that they are from Allah and let him thank Him for that. And if it is the other, let him know they are from Satan and let him seek refuge with Allah". *(Bukhari)*

The Angels are Allah's Messengers to us--not only to bring revelations to the Prophets but to strengthen directly the spiritual dimension of every man and woman by inspiring what is good. Neither they nor Satan are perceived by the senses of ordinary people, but we know they exist as we know our own existance although we cannot experience it physically. We experience our soul as an intangible, integrating and motivating force within ourselves. The Angels are experienced by us as intangible but unmistakable beings in the sense of shame that comes to us when we are about to act wrongly, and also as that flash of understanding when we dwell on godly thoughts or that sense of joy that accompanies a righteous act.

This *hadith* was said by the Prophet (Peace and blessings of Allah be upon him) immediately before he received the revelation:

$$ اَلشَّيْطَٰنُ يَعِدُكُمُ الْفَقْرَ وَيَأْمُرُكُم بِالْفَحْشَآءِ ۖ وَاللَّهُ يَعِدُكُم مَّغْفِرَةً مِّنْهُ وَفَضْلًا ۗ وَاللَّهُ وَاسِعٌ عَلِيمٌ ۝ $$

"Satan holds out to you the threat of poverty and bids you unto indecency and Allah promises you forgiveness from Himself and bounty (too). And Allah is Bounteous, All-Knowing"   (Q. 2:268).

That the Satan frightens you that if you spend in the cause of Allah, your wealth would be reduced and thus you would get into the grip of poverty. Satan not only threatens you with poverty but tempts you to adopt dishonest and immoral means to combat it.

Good and evil draw us opposite ways and by opposite

motives, and the contrast is well marked out in charity. When we think of doing some real act of kindness or charity we are assailed with doubts and ferar of impoverishment; but evil supports any tendency to selfishness, greed, or even to extravagant expenditure for show, or self-indulgence, or unseemly appetites. On the other hand Allah draws us on to all that is kind and good, for that way lies the forgiveness for our sins and greater real prosperity and saitsfaction. No kind or generous act ever ruined anyone. It is false generosity that is sometimes shown as leading to ruin. As Allah knows all our motives and cares for all, and has everything in His Power, it is the obvious course a wise man will choose. But wisdom is rare, and it is only wisdom that can appreciate true well-being and distinguish it from the false appearance of well-being.

The Prophet of Allah (peace and blessings of Allah be upon him) has instructed us to have faith in the existence of Allah's Angel. The article of Islamic faith is very important, because it absolves the concept of Tauhid for all impurities and frees it from the danger of conceivable shadow of *shirk* (polytheism).

The polytheists have associated two kinds of creatures with Allah:

a. Those who have material existence and are perceptible to the human eye, such as sun, moon, stars, fire, water, animals, great men.

b. Those who have no material existence and are not perceptible to the human eye: the unseen beings who are believed to be engaged in the administration of the universe; for instance, one controls the air, another imparts light, another brings rains, and so on and so forth.

The alleged deities of the first kind have material existence and are before man's eye. The falsity of their claim has been fully

exposed by the first Kalimah-----*La Ilaha illallah*. This is sufficient to dispose of the idea that they enjoy any share in divinity or
deserve any reverence at all. The second kind of things, being
immaterial, are hidden from the human eye and are mysterious; the
polytheists are more inclined to pin their faith in them. They
consider them to be deities, gods and god's children. They make
their images and render offerings to them. In order to purify belief
in the Unity of God, and to clear it from the admixture of this second
kind of unseen creatures, this particular article of faith has been
expounded.

The Prophet of Allah(peace and blessings of Allah be upon
him)has informed us that these imperceptible spiritual beings
whom people believe to be deities or gods or god's children, are
really His Angels. They have no share in Allah's divinity; they
cannot deviate from His commands even by the slightest fraction
of an inch. Allah employes them to administer His kingdom, and
they carry out His orders exactly and accurately. They have no
authority to do anything of their own accord; they cannot present
to Allah any scheme conceived by themselves, they are not even
authorised to intercede with Allah for any man.

To worship them and to solicit their help is degrading and
debasing for man. For on the very first day on man's creation, Allah
Almighty had made them prostrate themselves before Adam,
granted to him greater knowledge than they possessed and
bestowed on Adam his own vicegerency on this earth in preference
to them. What debasement can, therefore, be greater for man than
prostrating himself before those who had prostrated themselves
before him.

Mohammed (peace and blessings of Allah be upon him)
forbade us to worship Angels, and to associate them with Allah and
His divinity. He also informed us that they were the chosen

creatures of Allah, free from sin, from their very nature unable to disobey Allah, and ever engaged in carrying out His orders. Moreover, he informed us that these Angels of Allah surrounded us from all sides, are attached to us, and are always in our company. They observed and note all actions, good or bad. They preserve a complete record of every man's life. After death, when we shall be brought before Allah they will present a full report of our life's work on earth, wherein we shall find everything correctly recorded, not a single movement left out, however insignificant and however carefully concealed it may be.

We have not been informed of the intrinsic nature of the Angels. Only some of their virtues or attributes have been mentioned to us, and we have been asked to believe in their existence. We have no other means of knowing their nature, their attributes and their qualities. It would, therefore, be a sheer folly on our part to attribute any form or quality to them of our own accord. We must believe in them exactly as we have been asked to do. To deny their existence is *kufr* for, fisrt, we have no reason for such a denial, and, second, our denial of them would be tantamount to attribute untruth to Mohammed (peace and blessings of Allah be upon him). We believe in their existence only because Allah's true Messenger has informed us of it.

Allah Almighty says:

لَيْسَ الْبِرّ أَن تُوَلُّوا وُجُوهَكُمْ قِبَلَ الْمَشْرِقِ وَ الْمَغْرِبِ وَلَكِنَّ الْبِرَّمَنْ آمَنَ بِاللهِ وَالْيَوْمِ الْآخِرِ وَالْمَلَئِكَةِ وَالْكِتْبِ وَالنَّبِيِّنَ

"Virtue is not (this) that you turn your faces to the East or the West, but virtue is of him who believeth in Allah and the Last Day, and the Angels and the Book, and the Prophets...."

(Q. 2:177).

That is, the first requirement of true piety is the right belief in Allah, and the Last Day, and the Angels, and the Books and His Prophets. The order of the different articles of belief is very significant. Belief in Allah implies that one should also believe that Allah has not created human beings as mere playthings but He has created them as responsible beings who are held accountable to Him for all their deeds and misdeeds.

Then it is through his Angels that His commands are executed and the revelations are delivered to the Prophets. These revelations contain the Will of Allah and these are unerring guides to humanity. As all these Truths are made known to man through one agency- -Prophethood, the mention of the Prophets has, therefore, been made at the end. The idea behind it is to show that it is through the Prophets that we learn the true beliefs and the code of right conduct.

Allah Almighty once again says:

اٰمَنَ الرَّسُوْلُ بِمَآ أُنْزِلَ اِلَيْهِ مِنْ رَّبِّهِ وَ الْمُؤْمِنُوْنَ كُلٌّ اٰمَنَ بِاللّٰهِ وَمَلٰٓئِكَتِهِ وَكُتُبِهِ وَرُسُلِهِ ۟

"The Messenger believes in what is sent down to him from his Lord, and so do believers. Each one believes in Allah and His Angels and His Books, and His Messengers...."
(Q. 2:285).

Allah Almighty also says:

يٰٓاَيُّهَا الَّذِيْنَ اٰمَنُوْٓا اٰمِنُوْا بِاللّٰهِ وَرَسُوْلِهِ وَالْكِتٰبِ الَّذِيْ نَزَّلَ عَلٰى رَسُوْلِهِ وَالْكِتٰبِ الَّذِيْٓ اَنْزَلَ مِنْ قَبْلُ وَمَنْ يَّكْفُرْ بِاللّٰهِ وَمَلٰٓئِكَتِهِ وَكُتُبِهِ وَرُسُلِهِ وَالْيَوْمِ الْاٰخِرِ فَقَدْ ضَلَّ ضَلٰلًا بَعِيْدًا ۟

"O ye who believe! Affirm faith in Allah, and His Messengers and the Book that He has sent down unto His Messenger, and the Book that He sent down aforetime; and whosoever disbelieves in Allah, and His Angels, and His Books, and His Messengers, and the Last Day, has surely strayed far away." (Q. 4:136).

The supreme fact is again instilled into the minds of people that it is through right belief in Allah and His Messengers and His Books and His Angels that one can attain salvation and righteous act can emanate from the right belief only.

Created from Light

During the age of ignorance and darkness there was a lot of difference regarding the substance the Angels are created from and their sex.

Hazrat Ayesha (may Allah be pleased with her) is reported to have said

"The Angels were created from "light". The *jinn* were created from "fire". Man was created from what has been described to you". *(Muslim)*.

Hazrat Sa'eed bin al-Musayyab (may Allah be pleased with him) is reported to have said:

"The Angels are neither male or female. They neither eat nor drink. They do not marry nor have children." (Ibn Hajr in the Faith mentioned in *Rabi'al-Abrar*).

Regarding the sex of angels Allah Almighty says:

وَجَعَلُوا الْمَلَٰئِكَةَ يَقْسِمُونَ رَحْمَتَ رَبِّكَ نَحْنُ قَسَمْنَا بَيْنَهُمْ مَعِيشَتَهُمْ فِي الْحَيَوٰةِ شَهَادَتُهُمْ وَيُسْئَلُونَ ۝

"And they make into female angels who themselves serve

Allah. Did they witness their creation? Their evidence will be recorded, and they will be called to account: (Q. 43:19).

Angels for grace and purity may be compared to the most graceful and the purest forms we know. But it is wrong to attribute sex to them. They are "servants" and "Messengers" of Allah and so far from being rivals seeking worship, are always engaged in devotion and service. If any person invents blasphemies about Allah, such blesphemies will form a big blot in their Book of Deeds, and they wil be called to account for them.

Allah Almighty called the Angels "slaves" or "servants" and honoured them by the fact of their being connected to His name, the all-Merciful. He made it clear that those who think that they are female are not right because they say this with no knowledge.

Allah Almignty further says:

إِنَّ الَّذِينَ لَا يُؤْمِنُونَ بِالْآخِرَةِ لَيُسَمُّونَ الْمَلَٰئِكَةَ تَسْمِيَةَ الْأُنْثَىٰ

"Those who believe not in the Hereafter, name the Angels with female names"   (Q. 53:27).

To show Allah in human shape, or imagine sons or daughters of Allah, as if Allah were flesh, was in any case a derogation from the supreme glory of Allah, high above all creatures, even if the human shapes were invested with great beauty and majesty as in the Greek Pantheon. But when we consider in what low opinion Pagan Arabs held the female sex, it was particularly degrading to show Them, as so-called daughters of Allah in female shape.

Allah Almighty reveals:

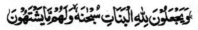

(a) "And they assign daughters for Allah;---Glory be to Him; And for themselves what they desire:

وَإِذَا بُشِّرَ أَحَدُهُم بِالأُنثَى ظَلَّ وَجْهُهُ مُسْوَدًّا وَهُوَ كَظِيمٌ ۝

(b) "When news is brought to one of them, of (the birth of) a female (child), his face darkens, and his filled with inward grief,"

يَتَوَارَى مِنَ الْقَوْمِ مِن سُوءِ مَا بُشِّرَ بِهِ أَيُمْسِكُهُ عَلَى هُونٍ أَمْ
يَدُسُّهُ فِي التُّرَابِ أَلَا سَاءَ مَا يَحْكُمُونَ

(c) "With shame does he hide himself from his people, because of the bad news he has had; shall he retain it on (sufferance and) contempt, or bury it in the dust? Ah; what an evil (choice) they decide on?" (Q. 16:59).

Allah Almighty has also said:

وَقَالُوا اتَّخَذَ الرَّحْمَنُ وَلَدًا سُبْحَانَهُ بَلْ عِبَادٌ مُّكْرَمُونَ

"And they say: 'The Most Gracious has taken a son; Glory to Him; they are (but) servants raised to honour" (Q. 21:26).

This refers both to the Trinitarian superstition that Allah has begotten a son, and to the Arab superstition that the Angels were daughters of Allah. All such superstitions are derogatory to the glory of Allah. The Prophet and the Angels are no more than servants of Allah: they are raised high in honour, and therefore they deserve our highest respect, but not our worship.

Some of the Pagan Arabs called Angels the daughters of Allah. In their own life they hated to have daughters. They practised female infanticide. In their state of perpetual war sons were a source of strength to them; daughters only made them subject to humiliating raids!

Here the practice of female infanticide is condemned in scathing terms. Female children used to be burried alive by the

Pagan Arabs.

The Number and Types of Angels

Allah Almighty says:

$$تَكَادُ السَّمٰوٰتُ يَتَفَطَّرْنَ مِنْ فَوْقِهِنَّ وَالْمَلٰٓئِكَةُ$$
$$يُسَبِّحُوْنَ بِحَمْدِ رَبِّهِمْ وَيَسْتَغْفِرُوْنَ لِمَنْ فِى الْاَرْضِ اَلَآ اِنَّ$$
$$اللهَ هُوَ الْغَفُوْرُ الرَّحِيْمُ$$

"The heavens are almost rent asunder from above them (by His Glory) : And the Angels celebrate the Praises of their Lord and pray for forgiveness for all beings on earth : Behold! Verily Allah is He, Oft-Forgiving, Most Merciful."
(Q. 42:5).

That is, how can we conceive of sublimity and greatness in a higher degree than this, that the highest heavens are almost ready to burst asunder by His Glory, which is higher than all? The Angels are the noblest and purest beings of whom we can conceive. They reflect on the one side Allah's Glory and Praise, and on the other, two other attributes of Allah, that look towards His erring creatures, viz., Forgiveness and Mercy. The two sets of attirbutes are complementary. They thus proclaim in their own being and in their prayers the Greatness and unbounded Goodness of Allah.

And Allah Almighty says:

$$وَمَا جَعَلْنَآ اَصْحٰبَ النَّارِ اِلَّا مَلٰٓئِكَةً وَّمَا جَعَلْنَا عِدَّتَهُمْ$$
$$اِلَّا فِتْنَةً لِّلَّذِيْنَ كَفَرُوْا لِيَسْتَيْقِنَ الَّذِيْنَ اُوْتُوا الْكِتٰبَ$$
$$وَيَزْدَادَ الَّذِيْنَ اٰمَنُوْآ اِيْمَانًا وَّلَا يَرْتَابَ الَّذِيْنَ اُوْتُوا$$

الْكِتَبَ وَالْمُؤْمِنُوْنَ وَلِيَقُوْلَ الَّذِيْنَ فِى قُلُوبِهِمْ مَّرَضٌ
وَّالْكِفِرُوْنَ مَاذَآ اَرَادَاللّٰهُ بِهٰذَا مَثَلًا كَذَٰلِكَ يُضِلُّ
اللّٰهُ مَنْ يَّشَآءُ وَيَهْدِىْ مَنْ يَّشَآءُ وَمَا يَعْلَمُ جُنُوْدَ
رَبِّكَ اِلَّا هُوَ وَمَا هِىَ اِلَّا ذِكْرٰى لِلْبَشَرِ ۞

"And We have set none but Angels as guardians of the Fire;
and We have fixed their number only as a trial for Unbelievers,--in order that the People of the Book may arrive at
certainty, and the Believers may increase in Faith------and
that no doubts may be left for the People of the Book and
the Believers, and that those in whose hearts is a disease and
the Unbelievers may say, "What doth Allah intend by this?"
Thus doth Allah leave to stray whom He pleaseth, and guide
whom He pleaseth and none can know the forces of thy
Lord, except He, and this is no other than a reminder to
mankind."   (Q. 74:31).

The figure nineteen refers to Angels appointed to guard Hell.

Moreover, there was a great volume of angelology in the
religious literature of the People of the Book (i.e., the Jesus and the
Christians) to whom (among others) an appeal is made in the verse.
The Essenes, a Jewish brotherhood with highly spiritual ideas; to
which perhaps the Prophet Jesus himself belonged, had an extensive literature of angelology. In the Midras also, which was a Jewish
school of exegesis and mystical interpretation, there was much said
about Angels. The Eastern Christian sects contemporary with the
birth of Islam had borrowed and developed many of these ideas,
and their mystics owed much to the gnostics and the Persian
apocalyptic systems. In the New Testament the relation of the
Angels with Fire is referred to more than once. In Rev. IX. 11 we
have "the angel of the bottomless pit, whose name in the Hebrew
tongue is Abaddon, but in the Greek tongue hath his name
Apollyon." In Rev. XIV. 18 there is an "angel which had power

over fire". And in Rev. XVI. 8 an angel has "power", given unto him to scorch men with fire." In the old Testament (Daniel VII. 9-10) the essence of all Angels in fire : thousands of them issued as a fiery stream from before the Ancient of Days, whose "throne was like the fiery flame, and His feels as burning fire".

The significance of numbers is a favourite theme with some writers, but I lay no stress on it. In Christian theology the number of the Beast, 666, in Rev. XIII. 18 has given rise to much controversy, and may refer only to the numerical value of the letters in the name of the Roman Emperor Nero.

There are four classes of people mentioned here.

(1) The Muslims will have their faith increased, because they believe that all revelation is from Allah Most Merciful and all His forces will work in their favour.

(2) The People of the Book, those who had received previous revelations of an analogous character, the Jews and Christians had numerous sects disputing with each other on minute points of doctrine; but they will now, if they believe, find rest from controversies in a broad understandings of scripture.

(3) Those in whose hearts is a disease, the insincere ones, the hypocrites, will only be mystified, because they believe nothing and have rejected the grace and mercy of Allah. Hypocrites are true to themselves, and therefore their hearts are diseased. The disease tends to spread, like all evil. They are curable but if they harden their hearts, they also pass into the category of those who deliberately reject light. The insincere man who thinks he can get the best of both worlds by compromising with good and evil only increases the disease of his heart, because he is not true to himself. Even the good which comes to him he can pervert to evil. So the rain which fills out the ear of corn or lends fragrance to the rose also lends strength to

the thorn or adds strength to the poison of the deadly night-shade.

Much mischief is caused (sometimes unwittingly) by people who think that they have a mission of peace, when they have not even a true perception of right and wrong. By their blind arrogance they depress the good and encourage the evil. A deeper phase of insincerity is actual duplicity. But it never pays in the end. If we compare such a man to a trader he loses in the bargain.

There are Angels without number and no one knows their number except for Him Who created them. If anyone has an idea of knowing their strength he should see the following *hadith*. The Prophet of Allah (peace and blessings of Allah be upon him) said:

> "The heaven groans and it has a right to groan. On the Day of Judgement Hell will be drawn up by 70,000 thongs and holding each thong there will be 70,000 angels" *(Ibn Majah)*.

According to that, the Angels who bring Hell on the Day of Resurection will alone number 4,900,000,000.

If you reflect on the texts related about the Angels who take care of each number of mankind, you will understand the hugeness of their number. There is the Angel in charge of each Semen drop, two Angels to record good and bad deeds of people, the guardian Angels, and also the two Angels accompanying each human being to guide and direct him to the right path.

The Wings of the Angels

Allah Almighty says:

الْحَمْدُ لِلّٰهِ فَاطِرِ السَّمٰوٰتِ وَالْأَرْضِ جَاعِلِ الْمَلٰٓئِكَةِ رُسُلًا أُولِىٓ أَجْنِحَةٍ مَّثْنٰى وَثُلٰثَ وَرُبٰعَ يَزِيْدُ فِى الْخَلْقِ مَا يَشَآءُ إِنَّ اللّٰهَ عَلٰى كُلِّ شَىْءٍ قَدِيْرٌ

"Praise be to Allah, the Originator of the heavens and the earth, Who made the Angels messengers with wings, --- two, or three, or four (pairs) : He adds to creation as He pleases : for Allah has power over all things"   (Q. 35:1).

That is, when we praise Allah, it means that we understand and bring to mind that His glory and power are exercised for the good of His Creation.

As man's knowledge of the process of nature advances, he sees how complex is the evolution of matter itself, leaving out the question of the origin of Life and the spiritual forces, which are beyond experimental science. But this knowledge itself becomes a sort of "veil of Light" : man become so conscious of the proximate causes that he is apt, in his pride, to forget the primal cause, the ultimate hand of Allah in Creation. And then, creation is such a complex process : see some of the ideas involved explained by different words. The word *fatara* here used means the creation of primeval matter, to which further creative processes have to be added by the hand of Allah, or Allah "adds to His Creation as He pleases", not only in quantity, but in qualities, functions, relations and variations in infinite ways.

These Angels are Messengers of Instruments of Allah's Will and may have a few or numerous Errands entrusted to them.

Allah Almighty makes it clear that the Angels have wings. Some of them have two wings, some three, some four, and some have more than that as has come in a *hadith* saying that Messenger of Allah (peace and blessings of Allah be upon him) saw Jibril (Gabriel) (peace be upon him) on the Night Journey and he had six hundred wings, the distance between each wing being the same as that between the East and the West.

Size of the Angels

Allah Almighty says:

يَـٰٓأَيُّهَا ٱلَّذِينَ ءَامَنُوا۟ قُوٓا۟ أَنفُسَكُمْ وَأَهْلِيكُمْ

نَارًا وَقُودُهَا ٱلنَّاسُ وَٱلْحِجَارَةُ عَلَيْهَا مَلَـٰٓئِكَةٌ غِلَاظٌ شِدَادٌ

لَّا يَعْصُونَ ٱللَّهَ مَآ أَمَرَهُمْ وَيَفْعَلُونَ مَا يُؤْمَرُونَ ۝

"O ye who believe! Save yourselves and your families from a Fire whose fuel is Men and Stones, over which are (appointed) angels stern (and) severe, who flinch not (from executing) the commands they receive from Allah, but do (precisely) what they are commanded" (Q. 66:6).

Note how we have been gradually led up in admonition from two consorts to all consorts, to all women, to all believers, and to all men and women. We must carefully guard not only our own conduct, but the conduct of our families, and of all who are near and dear to us. For the issues are most serious and the consequences of a faith are most terrible.

This is a terrible fire: not merely like the physical fire which burns wood or charcoal or substances like that , and consumes them. This Fire will have for its fuel men who do wrong and are as hard-hearted as stones, or stone idols as symbolical of all the unbending Falsehoods in life.

We think of the Angel's nature as gentle and beautiful, but in another aspect perfection includes justice, fidelity, discipline, and the firm execution of duty according to lawful commands. So, in the attributes of Allah Himself, Justice and Mercy, Kindness and Correction are not contradictory but complementary. An earthly ruler will be unkind to loyal subjects if he does not punish evildoers

Abdullah ibn Mas'ud (may Allah be pleased with him) is reported to have said:

"The Messenger of Allah (peace and blessings of Allah be upon him) saw Jibril (peace be upon him) in a green robe and he completely filled all the space between heaven and earth."

(Muslim)

The Messenger of Allah (peace and blessings of Allah be upon him) is reported to have said:

"I was given permission to speak about one of the Bearers of the Throne--his two feet are resting on the lowest earth and the Throne rests on the top of his head. The distance between his ear-lobes and his neck is that of the flight of a bird for seven hundred years. He (i.e. the Angel) says, `Glory be to you where-ever You are."

The Angels vary in size, not being all the same, some of them having two wings, some three, and some four up to Jibril who has six hundred wings.

Beautiful Form

Allah Almighty created the Angels with a beautiful form. He says:

$$ ذُو مِرَّةٍ فَاسْتَوَى ﴿ ﴾ $$

"Endued with Wisdom: for he appeared (in stately form)."

(Q. 53:6)

Abdullah Ibn Abbas (may Allah be pleased with him) said that dhu marra in this *ayah* means "having a beautiful appearance." It is commonly established knowledge that the Angels are beautiful in form, just as it is also commonly established that Satans are ugly. That is why people say that a beautiful human being looks like an Angel. Look at what the women said about Yusuf when they saw him:

The Holy Qur'an says:

فَلَمَّا رَأَيْنَهُ أَكْبَرْنَهُ وَقَطَّعْنَ أَيْدِيَهُنَّ وَقُلْنَ حَاشَ لِلّهِ مَا هَذَا بَشَرًا
إِنْ هَذَا إِلَّا مَلَكٌ كَرِيمٌ

"When they saw him, they did extol him, and (in their amazement) cut their hands: they said, `Allah preserve us! no mortal is this! This is none other than a noble Angel!"

(Q. 12:31)

That is when her reputation began to be pulled to pieces, the wife of Aziz invited ladies in society to a grand banquet. We can imagine them reclining at ease after the manner of fashionable banquets. When desert was reached and the talk flowed freely about the gossip and scandal which made their hostess interesting they were just about to cut the fruit with their knives, when, behold! Joseph (Yusuf) was brought into their midst, imagine the consternation which his beauty caused, and the havoc it played with their hearts! "Ah!" thought the wife of Aziz "now is your hypocrisy self-exposed! what about your reproaches to me? You have yourselves so lost your self-control that you have cut your fingers!"

Duties and the Worship of the Angels

Allah Almighty says:

وَتَرَى الْمَلَئِكَةَ حَآفِّينَ مِنْ حَوْلِ الْعَرْشِ يُسَبِّحُونَ بِحَمْدِ
رَبِّهِمْ وَقُضِىَ بَيْنَهُم بِالْحَقِّ وَقِيلَ الْحَمْدُ لِلّهِ رَبِّ الْعَلَمِينَ ۝

"And thou wilt see the Angels surrounding the Throne (Divine) on all sides, singing Glory and Praise to their Lord. The Decision between them (at Judgement) will be in (perfect) justice, and the cry (on all sides) will be, "Praise be to Allah, the Lord of the Worlds!"   (Q. 39:75)

Allah Almighty says that the Angels say:

$$\text{وَّإِنَّالَنَحْنُ الصَّآفُّونَ ۞ وَإِنَّالَنَحْنُ الْمُسَبِّحُونَ}$$

"And we are verily ranged in ranks (for service). And we are verily those who declare (Allah's) Glory!" (Q. 37:165-166).

That is, the Angels have been arranged in a heirarchy, like all servants of Allah. Just as human beings have individual talents and abilities which differentiate the nature of their work for Allah, so do the Angels. They are equal in rights, but they each have a prescribed duty to fulfil in the heavenly realm and in the earthly realm. In the spiritual world an Angel worships Allah through an alloted task and place, such as Throne-bearing, Gate-keeping or Fire supervision. And in the physical world he worships Allah Almighty through supervision of an assigned sphere, which is the limit of his knowledge and influence. This may be care of the rain, wind or stars, or it may be as a recorder of men's deeds or as bearer of the Revelation. The Holy Qur'an says:

"Those who bear the Throne (of Allah) and those around it sing Glory and Praise to their Lord; believe in Him; and implore Forgiveness for those who believe: "Our Lord! Thou embracest all things in Mercy and Knowledge. Forgive then those who turn in Repentance, and follow Thy Path; and preserve them for the Chastisement of the Blazing Fire!"

Jabir (may Allah be pleased with him) is reported to have said:

"The Messenger of Allah (peace and blessings of Allah be

upon him) said, `There is no space in the seven heavens a foot's length or a hand-span or a palm's width which does not have an Angel standing, bowing or prostrating on it." *(Tibrani)*.

It is confirmed in the two **Sahih** collections that the Messenger of Allah (peace and blessings of Allah be upon him) said in the *hadith* of the Night Journey after his visit to the seventh heaven:

> "Then I was taken up to the Frequented House and every day 70,000 angels visit it, never returning to it again, another (group) coming after them." (confirmed by two **Sahih** collections)

That is, the Angels worship and go round (**tawaf**) there just as the people of the earth do *tawaf* of their **K'aba**.

Al-`Awfi reports from Ibn Abbas (may Allah be pleased with him):

> "It is a house opposite the Throne. The Angels visit it and pray in it, 70,000 Angels every day, and never return to it again."

That is similar to what `Ikrama, Mujahid and several of the **Salaf** said.

About their obedience and dutifulness the Holy Qur'an says:

> "They speak not before He speaks, and they act (in all things) by His command. He knows what is before them, and what is behind them, and they offer no intercession except for those with whom He is well-pleased and they stand in awe and reverence of His (Glory).

The Angels are creation of Allah Almighty and are, therefore, His servants, just as we are--with the difference that their obedience is perfect, unquestioning, and without intermission, because of the nature Allah has given them. They never say anything before they receive Allah's command to say it, and their acts are similarly conditioned. This is also the teaching of Jesus as reported in the Gospel of St. John (xii. 49-50): "For I have not spoken of myself: but the "Father" which sent me, He gave me a commandment, what I should say, and what I should speak. And I know that His commandment is life-everlasting: whatsoever I speak therefore, even as the "Father" said unto me, so I speak". If rightly understood, "Father" has the same meaning as our *Rabb*, Sustainer and Cherisher, not Begetter or Progenitor.

Jibril (Gabriel)

Angels are the greatest and the mightiest creation of Allah Almighty and they have been entrusted with different duties and responsibilities. They all are blessed beings of Allah, the Creator and they never fail in their duties because they are quite above human weakness.

Hadrat Jibril (Gariel), peace be upon him, is entrusted with conveying the revelation from Allah Almighty to His Messengers (peace and blessings of Allah be upon thim).

The Holy Qur'an says:

نَزَلَ بِهِ الرُّوحُ الْأَمِينُ ۝ عَلَى قَلْبِكَ لِتَكُونَ مِنَ الْمُنْذِرِينَ ۝ بِلِسَانٍ عَرَبِيٍّ مُّبِينٍ

"With it came down the Truthful Spirit to thy heart that thou mayest admonish in the perspicuous Arabic tongue"
(Q. 26:193-195).

Ruh-Ul-Amin, the epithet of Gabriel, who came with the inspired Messages to the Holy Prophet, is difficult to render in a single epithet in translation. *Amin* is one to whom a trust has been given with several shades of meaning implied e.g.,

(a) worthy of trust,

(b) bound to deliver his trust, as a Prophet is bound to deliver His Message,

(c) bound to act entirely as directed by the trust, as a Prophet is bound to give only the Message of Allah and not add anything of his own, and

(d) not seeking any interest of his own.

A further signification as attached to the Spirit of inspiration is that it is the very quintessence of Faith and Truth, unlike the lying spirits which delude men with falsehood.

Qalb (Heart) signifies not only the seat of the affections, but also the seat of the memory and understanding. The process of inspiration is indicated by the impression of the Divine Message on the inspired one's heart, memory, and understanding, from which it was promulgated in human speech to the world. In this case the human speech was the perspicuous Arabic tongue, which would be plainly intelligible to the audience who would immediately hear it and through them transmitted to all the world.

Hadrat Ibn Abbas (may Allah be pleased with him) reports that the Messenger of Allah (peace and blessings of Allah be upon him) asked Jibril (peace be upon him) :

"What is Mika'il in charge of? "

"The plants and the rain" he replied"   *(Tibrani)*

Imam Ahmad reports from Anas bin Malik (may Allah be pleased with him) that the Messenger of Allah (peace and blessings of Allah be upon him) asked Jibril (peace be upon him):

"Why do I never see Mika'il laugh?"

"Mika'il has not laughed since the Fire was created", he replied.

There are several accounts of the way the revelation started to come to the Messenger of Allah (peace and blessings of Allah be upon him)

Ibn Shihab az-Zuhri reports that Urwa bin az-Zuhri had related to him that Hadrat Ayesha (may Allah be pleased with her) said:

"The beginnings of revelation to the Messenger of Allah (peace and blessings of Allah be upon him) took the form of true dreams. Whenever he had this kind of dream, it was something like the break of day. Then he was made to love going into retreat and used to retire to the cave `Hira' where he ould devote himself to the worship of Allah alone, continuing in this worship for a number of nights until he felt inclined to return to his family. He would take provisions for his stay. Then he would return to Khadija to restock with provisions and do the same again. This lasted until the Truth came to him while he was in the cave of Hira. The angel came to him and said, `Read!' he said, `I cannot read'. The Prophet (peace and blessings of Allah be upon him) said, `He seized me and squeezed me until all the strength went out of me and then released me and said, "Read!" I said, "I cannot read".

"Then he seized me and squeezed me a second time until all the strength went out of me and then released me then he seized me and squeezed me a third time and then released me, and then he said:

"Read in the name of your Lord who created man from a blood clot. Read, and your Lord is the Most Benevolent one"   (Q. 96: 1-3)

Dizzy and frightened by the strange experience which had never happened to him earlier nor had he ever heard about it, the Messenger of Allah (peace and blessings of Allah be upon him) came back with the verses, his heart trembling, and went to Khadija and said:

"Wrap me up, wrap me up", for he still felt fear for himself.

Khadija asked the reason for the Prophet's restlessness and the latter told her what had happened. Khadija was intelligent and prudent and had heard a great deal about the Messengers of Allah, Prophethood and Angels from her cousin Waraqa bin Naufal (who had embraced Christianity and read the Torah and Gospel). She was herself dissatisfied with the pagan cult of the Makkans like several other enlightened persons who had broken away from the idol worshippers.

Khadija was wife of the Prophet of Allah (peace and blessings of Allah be upon her). She had spent many years with him as the closest companion and knew him like the back of one's hand. By that alliance, Khadija was most conversant with the noble character of her husband. Worthiness of his moral fibre had convinced her that succour of the Lord would in any case stand by such a man. She knew in her heart that the good grace of God could never suffer one so high-minded truth-loving, trustworthy and upright as her husband was, to be possessed by a Jinn or a devil, and so she assured him with overweening self-confidence: "By no means; I swear to God that He would never shame you. You join the ties of relationship, you speak the truth, you bear people's burdens, you help the destitutes, you entertain guests and you mitigate the pains and griefs suffered for the sake of truth."

Khadija had tried to comfort and encourage her husband of

her own knowledge and understanding. But the matter was serious and pressing. She knew no peace until she had consulted someone knowledgeable of the revealed religions, their history and scriptures and the life of earlier Prophets of Allah. She wished to know for sure what had befallen her husband.

Khadija knew that Waraqa bin Naufal was the man who could be of help in the matter. She took the Apostle to Waraqa and when the Prophet told him what he had seen and heard, Waraqa cried out, "Verily by Him in whose hand is Waraqa's soul, Lo, thou ist the Prophet of this people. There hath come unto thee the greatest **Namus**, who came unto Moses afortime. A time will come when you wilt be called a liar, the people willt maltreat thee, cast thee out and fight against thee." The Apostle was surprised to hear Waraqa's forebodings for he had always been received with courtesy and regards by his fellow citizens. They addressed him as the trustworthy and honest. Holding his breath in amazement, he demanded from Waraqa:

"What! Will they expell me?"

"Yes", replied Waraqa, "for no man has ever brought anything like what thou hast brought without being opposed and fought by his people---this hath always been so. If I live to see that day, I shall stand by thee."

The words "there hath come unto thee the greatest `Namus' who came to Musa......." refer to Hadrat Jibril (peace be upon him). Linguists say that linguistically the Namus, is someone with a good secret and the "jasus" is someone with an evil secret. Scholars agree that Jibril (peace be upon him) is called "Namus" and they agree that he is what is meant here.

Imam al-Hurawi said:

"He is called that because Allah Almighty singled him out for the unseen and revelations."

Jabir bin Abdullah (may Allah be pleased with him), speaking about the time when there was an interval in the revelation' reports that the Messenger of Allah (peace and blessings of Allah be upon him) said:

"While I was out walking, I suddenly heard a voice from heaven. I raised my eyes and there was the same Angel who hath come to me at Hira'. He was sitting on a chair between heaven and earth. I was afraid of him and returned home and said, wrap me up! wrap me up!" Then Allah Almighty sent down:

$$ يَا أَيُّهَا الْمُدَّثِّرُ ۝ قُمْ فَأَنْذِرْ ۝ وَرَبَّكَ فَكَبِّرْ ۝ وَثِيَابَكَ فَطَهِّرْ ۝ وَالرُّجْزَ فَاهْجُرْ $$

"O thou wrapped up (in a mantle)! Arise and deliver thy warning! And thy Lord do thou magnify! And thy garments keep free from stain! And all abomination shun!"(Q.74:1-5).

In these wonderful early verses there is a double thread of thought: (1) A particular occasion or person is referred to; (2) A general spiritual lessson is taught. As to (1), the Prophet was now passed the stage of personal contemplation, lying down or sitting in his mantle; he was now to go boldly to deliver his Message and publicly proclaim the Lord: his heart had always been purified, but now all his outward doings must be dedicated to Allah, and conventional respect for ancestral customs or worship must be thrown aside; his work as a Messenger was the generous gift that could flow from the personality, but no reward or appreciation was to be expected from his people, but quite the contrary; there would be much call on his patience, but his contentment would arise from the good pleasure of Allah. As to (2), similar stages arise in a minor degree in the life of every good man, for which the Prophet's life is to be a universal pattern.

Al-Bukhari transmitted in his **Sahih** from Hadrat Ayesha (may Allah be pleased with her), that al-Harith b. Hisham asked the Messenger of Allah (peace and blessings of Allah be upon him):

> "Messenger of Allah! How does the revelation come to you?"

> "Sometimes it comes to me like the ringing of a bell and this is the hardest on me--which then leaves me after I have fully understood and retained what was said. Sometimes the Angel comes to me in the form of a man and speaks to me and I retain what he says", the Messenger of Allah (peace and blessings of Allah be upon him) said.   *(Bukhari)*

Hadrat Ayesha (may Allah be pleased with her) is reported to hae said.

> "I saw him when the revelation was descending on him on a very cold day and when it left him his brow was dripping with perspiration."

Ibn al-Qayyim (may mercy of Allah be upon him) said that there were seven ways in which revelations came:

1) The first was the true dream. This was the beginning of revelation to the Prophet (peace and blessings of Allah be upon him). Whenever he had this kind of dream, it was clear like the break of day.

2) There was also what the Angel imparted to his soul and heart without seeing him. as Prophet (peace and blessings of Allah be upon him), said, "The Spirit of Purity imparted to my heart that no self dies until its provision is complete, so fear Allah and be

moderate in asking. Do not let delay of provision move you to seek it by disobeying Allah. What is with Allah is only obtained by obeying Him."

3) The third was that the Angel used to take on the form of a man to the Prophet (peace and blessings of Allah be upon him), and speak to him so that he remembered what he said to him. It is in this form the Companions used sometimes to see him.

4) Revelation used to come to him like the ringing of a bell. This was the hardest for him. The Angel would make it so difficult for him that his brow would drip either perspiration on even a very cold day and his camel would be forced into kneeling on the ground when he was riding it. On one occasion revelation came like that when his thigh was resting on the thigh of Zayd bin Thabit (may Allah be pleased with him) and it became so heavy that it nearly broke Zayd's thigh.

5) The fifth was that he saw the Angel in his true form and he would reveal to him whatever Allah Almighty wished to reveal to him. This occurred twice to the Prophet of Allah (peace and blessings of Allah be upon him), as Allah Almighty mentions in **Surah an-Najm**

6) The sixth was when Allah Almighty revealed things to him directly such as the obligation of the prayer and other things when he was above the heavens during the Night Journey.

7) The seventh were the words of Allah Almighty which came to Him without the intermediary of the Angel, in the same way that Allah spoke to Musa, son of `Imran. This kind of revelation is absolutely confirmed in the case of Musa by the text of the Qur'an and in the case of our Prophet (peace and blessings of Allah be upon him) in the hadith of the Night Journey.

Attributes

Allah Almighty says.

وَالنَّجْمِ إِذَا هَوَىٰ ۞ مَا ضَلَّ صَاحِبُكُمْ وَمَا غَوَىٰ ۞ وَمَا يَنطِقُ عَنِ الْهَوَىٰ ۞
إِنْ هُوَ إِلَّا وَحْىٌ يُوحَىٰ ۞ عَلَّمَهُ شَدِيدُ الْقُوَىٰ ۞ ذُو مِرَّةٍ فَاسْتَوَىٰ

"By the star when it goes down,--your Companion is neither
astray nor being misled, nor does he say (aught) of (his own)
Desire. It is no less that inspiration sent down to him: He was
taught by one Mighty in Power, endued with Wisdom: For
he appeared (in stately form) "   (Q 53:1-6).

Ibn al Qayyim (may Allah have mercy on him) says of these
ayahs: "Allah Almighty has described His angelic Messenger, Jibril
(peace be upon him), in this *surah* as being noble, strong, secure
with his Lord, obeyed in the heavens, and trustworthy. These five
qualities contain testimony of the trustworthiness of the *isnad* of the
Qur'an and that Mohammed (peace and blessings of Allah be upon
him) heard it from Jibril (peace be upon him), and that Jibril had it
from the Lord of the worlds. This *isnad* should be enough for you
in respect of sublimity and majesty.

"The first quality is that the Messenger who brought it to
Mohammed (peace and blessings of Allah be upon him),
had 'nobility'. This refutes the words of enemies about
Shaytan (Satan) being one who brought it. Satan is foul and
repulsive, vile, ugly and totally lacking in good. His inward
is more ugly than his outward and his outward more evil than
his inward. There is no good in him or with him. He is the
furthest thing from nobility. The messenger who brought the
Qur'an to Mohammed (peace and blessings of Allah be
upon him) was noble and of beautiful appearance. Allah
Almighty describes him in Surah an-Najm, as "**endowed**

with strength"

Ibn Abbas (may Allah be pleased with him) said that this means to have a beautiful appearance and radiant form, to be full of excellence, good and wholesomeness' teaching those who are good. Every good in the earth is from guidance, knowledge, gnosis and belief and piety. This is part of what Lord makes happen at his hand. This is the utmost degree of nobility in form and meaning.

"The second quality is "power", as Allah Almighty says in **Surah an-Najm**, "Taught by one terrible in power" that calls our attention to several things. One of them is that by his strength he prevents devils from coming near him and obtaining anything from him and adding to our detracting from it. Rather when Satan sees him, he flees from him and does not come near him. Second is that he is a supporter of the Messenger whom they denied and is his assistant, friend and helper whoever has this powerful one as his friend, helper, aide and teacher is the assisted guide and Allah is his guide and helper. Another is that anyone who opposes this Messenger also opposes his companion and friend, Jibril, and whoever opposes someone with power and force exposes himself to destruction. Yet another is that he is able to carry out what he is commanded to do on account of his power and is not incapable of doing it and conveying his trust as he was commanded. He is the Strong Trustee.

The third attirbute is in the words of Almighty "**secure with the Lord of the Throne**", i.e. he has position and standing with Him and is the nearest Angel to Him. It is indicated by His words, "with the Lord of the Throne", indicating the high position of Jibril (peace be upon him), since he was near to the Lord of the Throne.

The fourth attribute is in His word, "obeyed". This makes it clear that his troops and helpers obey him when he delegates them to help his companion and friend, Mohammed (peace and blessings of Allah be upon him). It contains an indication that Jibril is obeyed in the heavens and that both of the Messengers are obeyed in their respective places and by their people. It also shows esteem for him since he has the position of kings who are obeyed among their people. Allah Almighty did not appoint to this immense matter anyone other tham someone who would be obeyed like a king.

The fifth attribute is in the words of the Almighty, "**the trustworthy.**" His being described with trustworthiness contains an indication of the careful preservation of what he carried and of the fact that he conveyed it properly

Jews --- Enemy of Jibril

Tirmizi reports that the Jews said about the Prophet (peace and blessings of Allah be upon him):

"He is not one of the Prophets unless one of the Angels comes to him from the presence of his Lord with the message and revelation.

"Who is your companion that we should follow you?"

"Jibril", he said.

"He is our enemy! If you had said Mika'il (Michael) who brings down the rain and mercy, we would have followed you", they said. So Allah sent down His words:

قُلْ مَنْ كَانَ عَدُوًّا لِجِبْرِيْلَ فَإِنَّهُ نَزَّلَهُ
عَلَى قَلْبِكَ بِإِذْنِ اللهِ مُصَدِّقًا لِمَا بَيْنَ يَدَيْهِ وَهُدًى
وَّبُشْرَى لِلْمُؤْمِنِيْنَ ۞ مَنْ كَانَ عَدُوًّا لِلهِ وَمَلَئِكَتِهِ وَ
رُسُلِهِ وَجِبْرِيْلَ وَمِيْكٰلَ فَإِنَّ اللهَ عَدُوٌّ لِّلْكٰفِرِيْنَ۞

"Say (O Prophet) whosoever is an enemy to Jibril (Gabriel) --who brings down upon your heart (revelation) by Allah's command confirming what was (revealed) before it and a guidance, and glad tidings to the believers. Whosoever is an enemy to Allah and His Angels and His Messengers and Gabriel and Michael----verily Allah is the enemy to the un-believers."   (Q. 2:97-98).

Jibril is a compound word made of *Jabr* and *il* and means a servant of Allah. *Jabr* in Hebrew is *Gebr* which means a servant and it also means mighty; the Powerful. Gabriel being the chief amongst the Angels was the bearer of Qur'anic Revelation. He is also called as `**Ruh-ul-Qudus** and **Ruh-ul-Amin** in the Qur'an. According to the Bible the function of Gabriel is to convey the message of God to His servants (Luke, 1:19). The Jews however, looked upon Gabriel as the Angel of heavenly vengeance and fire and looked upon Michael as their national guardian and a messenger of peace and plenty.   (See Daniel Xii: and Vii: 16,17).

The word **idhn** signifies permission, leave or concession of liberty to do a thing, and some time command.

The Holy Qur'an states that this pretence that Michael is their friend and Gabriel is their enemy, so the revelation which has been vouchsafed to Mohammed (peace and blessings of Allah be upon him) through Gabriel is not acceptable to them reflects their perverted state of mind. Who are they to dictate Allah? The Angels are the loyal servants of Allah and they carry out His commands according to His will. None has, therefore, any right to challenge or find fault with the dispensation of Allah.

The Jews should also ponder that if Gabriel were really their enemy how could he bring such a revelation (Qur'an) which verified their Torah and their Prophets. There is an implied answer to the baseless charge of the Jews that Gabriel brings nothing but calamity. They are comforted by the fact that Gabriel is the harbinger of glad tidings for the believers. If he is a bearer of fear it is for the unbelievers and the disobedient.

The Qur'an makes it clear that hostility to anyone---be it Allah, or anyone of His Angels or His Messengers----is a manifestation of one's un-belief. When Allah is accepted as the Supreme Authority and the final Dispenser of all things one must accept His Will and His Scheme of things as the most correct and sublime, free from every fault or defect. This is the basic demand of one's belief in Allah. To believe in God and to pick holes in His dispensation are two contradictory attitudes.

So far as the enmity of man to Allah and that of Allah's to man is concerned, it should be clearly borne in mind that in reality there can be no enmity between Allah and man as man cannot stand even the slightest wrath of all-Powerful Lord. Here enmity of Allah to man indicates the privation which one would suffer in one's life for one's unbelief, and as its consequence punishment in the Hereafter. As regards man's enmity to Allah, it implies to His commandments.

According to Abdullah Yusuf Ali, a party of the Jews in the time of Mohammed (peace and blessings of Allah be upon him) ridiculed the Muslim belief that Gabriel brought down revelations to Mohammed Al-Mustafa. Michael was called in their books "the great prince which standeth for the children of thy people." (Daniel, Xii. 1). The vision of Gabriel inspired feared. (Daniel, Viii, 16,17). But their pretence---that Michael was their friend and Gabriel their enemy----was merely a manifestation of their unbelief in Angels, Prophets and Allah Himself, and such unbelief could not win the love of Allah. Mohammed's inspiration was through visions c Gabriel. Mohammed (peace and blessings of Allah be upon him) had been helped to the highest spiritual light, and the messages were manifest signs which everyone could understand except those who were obstinate and perverse. Besides, the verses of the Qur'an were in themselves reasonable and clear.

The jews claim that Jibril (peace be upon him) was their enemy and that this enmity is what prevented them from believing in the prophethood of Mohammed (peace and blessings of Allah be upon him), since the one who brought him the revelation was Jibril (peace be upon him). The truth is that their enmity to him stemmed from rancour and envy since they disliked the fact that prophethood had moved from them to this middle community and that Jibril (peace be upon him), had descended with the firm **deen** which obrogates other **deens**.

Almighty made it clear that the affair was not Jibril's. Rather the affair was Allah's entirely. That is why Allah Almighty says, "**He was the one who brought it down upon your heart, by the authority of Allah.**" i.e. Jibril the Trustee brought this Qur'an down on your heart, O Mohammed, by the command of Allah Almighty, "Confirming what came before it" of the divine books, and "**as guidance and good news for the believers**", i.e., it contains perfect guidance and delightful good news of the Garden of Bliss for the believers.

Al-Qurtabi said:

"The *ayah* indicates the honour of Jibril (peace be upon him), and the censure of all who oppose him. The words of the Almighty, "**Anyone who is an enemy of Allah and His Angels and His Messengers and Jibril and Mika'il, Allah is an enemy of the rejectors.**" is a threat and a rebuke to all opponents of Jibril (peace be upon him), and it informs us that enmity to some things necessarily entails Allah's enmity in return. The enmity of the slave in respect of Allah is to disobey Him and to avoid obeying Him, and to be hostile towards His friends. Allah's enmity to the slave is to punish him and to cause the effects of enmity to appear on him.

"If it is said: "Why did Allah single out Jibril and Mika'il for mention, when the mention of the Angels included them in any case?" the answer is that He singled out the mention of the two of them to honour them and also because the Jews had mentioned them in particular. They were therefore the direct cause of the *ayah* being sent down and it was necessary to mention them so that the Jews could not then say, `We did not oppose Allah and all His angels'. Thus Allah Almighty sent them both to counter the interpretation that they mighty make."

Mi'raj (Ascension of the Prophet of Allah)

Allah Almighty says:

سُبْحَنَ الَّذِى أَسْرَى بِعَبْدِهِ لَيْلاًمِّنَ الْمَسْجِدِ
الْحَرَامِ إِلَى الْمَسْجِدِ الْأَقْصَا الَّذِى بَرَكْنَا حَوْلَهُ لِنُرِيَهُ مِنْ
اٰيٰتِنَا إِنَّهُ هُوَ السَّمِيعُ الْبَصِيْرُ

"Glory to (Allah) who did take His servant for a Journey by night from the Sacred Mosque to the Farthest Mosque whose Precincts we did bless,---in order that We might show him some of Our Signs: for He is the one Who heareth and seeth all things."
(Q. 17:1)

Surah Isra or Bani Israil opens with the night journey of the Holy Prophet (peace and blessings of Allah be upon him): he was transported from the sacred Mosque (of Makkah) to the farthest Mosque (of Jerusalem) in a night and shown some of the Signs of

Allah. The majority of Commentators take this Night Journey literally. The *Hadith* literature gives details of this journey and its study helps elucidate its meaning. The Holy Prophet (peace and blessings of Allah be upon him) was first transported to the seat of the earlier revelations in Jerusalem, and then taken through the seven heavens even to the Sublime Throne. The Spaniard, Miduel Asin, Arabic Professor in the University of Madrid, has shown that this *Mi`raj* literature had a great influence on the great Italian poem, the **Divine Comedy** (or Drama) of Dante, which towers like a randmark in medieval.

The reference to this great story of the *Mi`raj* is a fitting prelude to the journey of the human soul in its religious growth in life. The first steps in such growth must be through moral conduct---the reciprocal rights of parents and children, kindness to our fellow- men, courage and firmness in the hour of danger, a sense of personal responsibility, and a sense of Allah's Presence through prayer and praise.

The *Miraj* is usually dated to the 27th night of month of Rajab.

Masjid is a place of prayer : here it refers to the K'aba at Makkah. It had not yet been cleared of its idols (as) rededicated exclusively to the one True God. It was symbolical of the new Message which was being given to mankind.

The **Farthest Mosque** must refer to the site of the temple of Soloman in Jerusalem on the hill of Moriah, at or near which stands the Dome of the Rock, called also the Mosque of Umar (may Allah be pleased with him). This and the Mosque known as the Farthest Mosque (Masjid-ul-Aqsa) were completed by Amir Abd-ul-Malik in A.H. 68. **Farthest**, because it was the place of worship farthest west which was known to the Arabs in the time of the Holy Prophet (peace and blessings of Allah be upon him): It was a sacred place to both Jews and Christians, but the Christians then had the upper hand, as it was included in the Byzantine (Roman) Empire, which mentioned a Patriarch at Jerusalem. The chief dates in connection with the Temple are: it was finished by Solomon about B.C. 1004, destroyed by the Babylonions under Nebuchadnezzar about 586 B.C. rebuilt under Ezra and Nehemiah about 515 B.C.; turned into a heathen idol temple by one of Alexander's successors, Antiochus Epiphanes, 167 B.C.; restored by Herod, B.C. 17 to A.D. 29; and completely razed to the ground by the Emperor Titus in A.D. 70. These ups and downs are among the greater Signs in religious history.

Muslims transmitted in his **Sahih** from Anas bin Malik that the Messenger of Allah (peace and blessings of Allah be upon him) said:

> "Buraq was brought to me, a tall white animal somewhat larger than donkey but smaller than a mule. Its hoof alights at the point reached by its glance" He said, "I mounted and rode it until I reached Jerusalem." He said that he tied it to the ring to which the Prophets tie their mounts."

He said, "I entered the Mosque and prayed two *raka'ahs* in it. Then I left and Jibril (peace and blessings of Allah be upon him) brought me a cup of wine and a cup of milk. I chose the milk and Jirbril said, You have chosen the natural way.'

> "Then he took me up to the lowest heaven and jibril asked for it to be opened. It was said,
> `Who are you?'
> `Jibril', he said.
> `Who is with you?' it was said.
> `Mohammed', he said.
> `Has he been sent for ?' it was said.
> `He has been sent for", he said.

So it was opened for us and there I found Adam. He greeted me and prayed for good for me and then took us upto the second heaven and Jibril (peace be upon him), asked for it to be opened.

'Who are you?' it was said.

'Jibril', he said.

'Who is with you?' it was said.

'Mohammed', he said.

'Has he been sent for?' it was said.

'He has been sent for', he said.

So it was opened for us and I found there my cousins Isa bin-Maryam and Yahya bin-Zakariya (peace be upon them). They greeted me and prayed for good for me and then took me upto the third heaven and Jibril asked for it to be opened.

'Who are you?' it was said.

'Jibril' he said.

'Who is with you?' it was said.

'Mohammed',

'Has he been sent for?' it was said.

'He has been sent for', he said.

So it was opened for us and I found there Idris. He greeted me and prayed for good for me. Allah Almighty says, '**We raised him upto high place**.'

"Then he took us upto the fifth heaven. Jibril asked for it to be opened.

'Who are you?' it was said.

'Jibril', he said.

'Who is with you?' it was asked.

'Mohammed', he said.

'Has he been sent for?' it was asked.

'He has been sent for', he said.

So it was opened for us. I found there Haroon. He greeted me and prayed for good for me. Then he took us to the sixth heaven and Jibril asked it to be opened.

`Who are you?' it was said.

`Jibril' he said.

`Who is with you?'

`Mohammed', he said.

`Has he been sent for?' it was said.

`He has been sent for', he said.

So it was opened for us and I fouund there Musa. He greeted me and prayed for good for me.

`Then he took us upto the seventh heaven. Jibril asked for it to be opened.

`Who are you?' it was said.

`Jibril', he said.

`Who is with you?' it was said.

`Mohammed', he said.

`Has he been sent for?' it was said.

`He has been sent for', he said.

So it was opened for us and I found myself with Ibrahim who was leaning with his back against the Frequented House. Every day 70,000 angels visit it, never returning to it again. Then he took me to the Lot Tree of Farthest Limit whose leaves were like elephant's ears and fruits were like earthware jugs.

He said, "When it was covered over by the command of Allah, a change came over it and nothing in Allah's creation would be able to describe it owing to its extreme beauty. Allah revealed to me what He revealed and made fifty prayers obligatory for me in every day and night. Then I went down to Musa who said,

`What did your Lord make obligatory for your community?'

`Fifty prayers!

`Go back to your Lord and ask him to reduce it. Your community will never be able to do that. I know by my experience of the tribe of Isra'el."

He said, "I went back to my Lord and said, `O Lord, reduce it for my community', and he reduced it for me by five. I went back to Musa and said, `He reduced it by five for me'. He said, "Your community will not be able to do it. Go back to your Lord and ask Him to reduce it." He said:

"I continued to go back and forth between my Lord, the Blessed and Exalted, and Musa and until he said, `O Mohammed, they are five prayers every day and night, but each prayer counts as ten so that makes fifty prayers. Whoever intends a good action and does not do it, a good action will be written down for him. If he does it, ten will be written down for him. Whoever intends an evil action and does not do it, nothing will be written against him. If he does it, one evil action will be written down."

He said, "I went back down to Musa, and informed him and he said, `Go back to our Lord and ask Him to reduce it.' The Messenger of Allah (may peace and blessings of Allah be upon him) said, "I said, `I have returned to my Lord so often that I am ashamed before Him."

An-Nawwi said in the commentary of this **hadith**, "The Qadi said that this **hadith** indicates that heaven has real gates with sentries guarding them, and it contains affirmation of the needs to ask permission before entering."

An-Nawwi said, "As for the words of the sentries of heaven, `Has he been sent for?' it means: `Have you been sent to him to conduct him on the Night Journey and ascend through the heavens.' It is not a question going back to the basis of the mission and the message."

The words of the Prophet (peace and blessings of Allah be upon him):

"Then he took me to the Lote Tree of the Farthest Limit."
occurs sometimes with the definite article (**as-Sidra al-Muntaha**), and in some variants as **Sidra al-Muntaha**. Ibn ' Abbas and the commentators and others said that it is called the Lote Tree of the Farthest Limit because the knowledge of the Angels stops there and no one was able to go beyond it except the Messenger of Allah (peace and blessings of Allah be upon him).

It is related from Ibn Mas'ud (may Allah be pleased with him) that it is called that because it is reached both by what comes down to it from above it and also by what comes up to it from underneath of the command of Allah Almighty.

It is desirable to quote the illuminating commentary of Maulana Syed Abul Hasan Ali Nadwi on the event of *Mi'raj:*

"It was during this period that the Prophet found himself transported at night to the *K'aba* and from there to the place of Solomon's Temple in Jerusalem, where now stands **Masjid-il-Aqsa**; and was then borne to the celestial regions where he witnessed the seven heavens, met the Prophets of yore and saw the remarkable signs of divine majesty about which the Qur'an says:

$$\text{مَازَاغَ الْبَصَرُ وَمَا طَغَى ۞ لَقَدْ رَأَى مِنْ اٰيٰتِ رَبِّهِ الْكُبْرَى}$$

"The eye turned not aside nor yet was overbold, verily he saw one of the greater revelations of his Lord."(Q.53:17-18)

"Occurence of the event at that time was meant to confer

dignity upon he Apostle; it signified something like viands of higher regale in order to console and alleviate the feelings of distress caused to him by the persecution of the pagans at Ta'if. On the morrow of ascent the Apostle told the people about his nocturnal journey, but the Quraysh mocked and shook their heads saying it was inconceivable and beyond the bounds of reason. When Abu Bakr saw the Qureysh accusing the Apostle of falsehood he said, "what makes you wonder about it? If he has said that, it must be true. By God, he tells me that revelation descends on Him from the Heaven in a trice during the day or night and I avouch him. This is even more unimaginable and difficult than what seems astound you."

(Ibn Kathir, vol. II, P 96, Ibn Hisham, vol. I, P. 339)."

"The ascent did not come off in a routine or ordinary run of things only to demonstrate the recondite phenomena of the Kingdom of God in the heavens and the earth to the Prophet of Islam. In addition to it, this prophetic journey of tremendous importance alludes to a number of other significant and abstruse realities of far-reaching concern to humanity. The two Surahs of Isra and An-Najam revealed in connection with this heavenly journey indicate that Mohammed (peace and blessings of Allah be upon him) was charged with the office of prophethood for both the houses of God, those in Jerusalem and Makkah, and was sent as the leader of the east and the west or the entire human race to the end of time. As the inheritor of all the Prophets of old, he represented the fulfilment of consumption of mankind's religious development. His nightly journey from Makkah to Jerusalem expresses, in a figurative way, that his personality alluded to the one-ness of Baitul-Haram and Masjid-il-Aqsa. That all the

Prophets arraingned themselves behind him in Masjid-il-Aqsa shows that the doctrine of Islam, preached by him, was final universal and all comprehensive meant for every class and section of human society through the ages.

The event is, at the same time, indicative of the comprehensiveness of the Holy Prophet's apostleship' the place accorded to his followers in the great task of humanity's guidance and the distinctive character of his message.

Truly speaking, the ascent of the apostleship represents a line of demarcation between the regional limited and variable rules of divine guidance entrusted to the Prophet of old and the global, comprehensive and abiding principles of faith vouchsafed to the universal leader of human race. Had the Apostle been a sectional or regional guide, a national leader, the saviour of any particular race or the restorer of the glory of any particular people, there would have been no need of honouring him with ascension to the heavens nor would he have been required to perceive the hidden phenomena of the Heavens and the earth. Nor would it have been necessary to create the new link between the celestial and the earthly surface of the divine Kingdom; in that case the confines of his own land, his surroundings, environs and the times would have been sufficient enough; and there would have then been no need for him to divert his attention to any other land or country. Neither his ascension to the most sublime regions of the Heaven and to the "Lote Tree of the Farthest Limit nor even the nocturnal journey to the far away Jerusalem, then in the grip of powerful Christian Empire of Byzantian, would have been necessary at all.

Ascension of the Apostle was a divine proclamation that he had nothing to do with the category of national or political leaders whose endeavours are limited to their own country and nation. For they serve the nations and races to which they belong and are a product of their time, they serve the need of a particular juncture. The Apostle of Islam, on the contrary, belonged to the luminous line of the Messengers of God who communicate the inspired message of the Heavens and the earth. They are the links between God and His creatures. Their message transcends the limitations of time and space, race and colour, country and nation, for they are meant for the exaltation of man regardless of his colour, race or country."   (Mohammad Rasulullah pp. 134-136).

The Orientlist Dermenghem has reported the following eloquent story called from a number of biography books. It is desirable to quote it hereunder:

"In the middle of a solemn quiet night when even the night-birds and the rambling beasts were quiet, when the streams had stopped murmuring and no breezes played, Mohammed was awakened by a voice crying: `Sleeper awake!' And before him stood the angel Gabriel with radiant forhead, countenance white as snow, blood hair floating, in garments sewn with pearls and embroidered in gold. Manifold wings of every colour stood our quivering from his body.

"He led a fantastical steed, *Boraq* (Lightening), with a human head and two Angels' wings; it approached Mohammed, allowed him to mount and was off like an arrow over the mountains of Makkah and the sands of the desert towards the North... the angel accompanied them on this prodigious flight. On the summit of Mt. Sinai, where God had spoken to Moses, Gabriel stoped Mohammed for prayer, and agian at Bethlehem where Jesus was born, before resuming their course in the air. Mysterious vioces attempted to detain the Prophet, who was so wrapped up in his mission that he felt God alone had the right to stop his steed. When they reached Jerusalem Mohammed tethered Boraq and prayed on the ruins of the Temple of Solomon with Abraham, Moses and Jesus. Seeing an endless ladder appear upon Jacob's rock, the Prophet was enabled to mount rapidly to the heavens.

"The first heaven was of pure silver and the stars suspended from its vault by chains of gold; in each one an angel lay awake to prevent the demons from climbing into the Holy dwelling places and the spirits from listening indiscreetly to celestial secrets. There, Mohammed greeted Adam. And in the six other heavens the Prophet met Noah, Aaron, Moses, Abraham, David, Solomon, Idrees, (Enoch) Yahya (John the Baptist) and Jesus. He saw the Angel of Death, Azrail, so huge that his eyes separated by 70,000 marching days. He commanded 100,000 battalions and passed his time in writing in an immense book the names of those dying or being born. He saw the angel of Tears who wept for the sins of the world; the Angel of vengeance with brazen face, covered with warts, who presides over the elements of fire and sits on a Throne of flames; and another immense Angel made up half of snow and half of fire surrounded by a heavenly choir continually crying: 'O God, Thou hast united snow and fire, united all Thy servants in obedience to Thy laws'. In the seventh heaven where the souls of the just resided was an Angel larger than the entire world, with 70,000 heads; each head had 70,000 mouths, each mouth had 70,000 tongues and each tongue spoke 70,000 different idioms singing endlessly the praises of the Most High.

"While contemplating this extraordinary being,

Mohammed was carried to the top of the Lote Tree of Heaven flowering at the right of God's invisible throne and shading myriads of angelic spirits. Then after having crossed in a twinkling of an eye the widest seas, regions of dazzlings light and deepest darkness, traveresed millions of clouds of hyacinths, of guaze, of shadows, of fire, of air, of water, of void, each one separated by 500 marching years, he then passed more clouds---of beauty, of perfection, of supremacy, immensity, of unity, behind which are 70,000 choirs of angels bowed down and motionless in complete silence. The earth began to heave and he felt himself caried into the light of his Lord, where he was transfixed, paralysed. From here heaven and earth together appeared as if imperceptible to hm, as if melted into nothingness and reduced to the size of a grain of mustard-seed in the middle of a field. And this is how Mohammed admits having been before the Throne of the Lord of the world.

"He was in the presence of the Throne `**at a distance of two bows length or yet nearer'**, behoding God with his soul's eyes and seeing things which the tongue cannot express, surpassing all human understanding. The Almighty placed one hand on Mohammed's breast and another on his shoulder---to the very marrow of his bones he felt an icy chill, followed by an inexpressible feeling of calm and ecstatic annihilation.

"After a conversion whose ineffability is not honoured by too precise tradition, the Prophet received the command from God that all believers must say fifty prayers each day. Upon coming down from heaven Mohammed met Moses, who spoke with him on this subject:

"How do you hope to make your followers say fifty

prayers each day? I had experience with mankind before you. I tried everything with the children of Israel that was possible to try. Take my word, return to our Lord and ask for a reduction.'

"Mohammed returned, and the number of prayers was reduced to forty. Moses thought that this was still too many and made his successor go back to God a number of times. In the end God exacted not more than five prayers.

"Gabriel then took the Prophet to paradise where the faithful rejoice after their resurrection -- an immense garden with silver soil, gravel of pearls, mountains of amber, filled with golden palaces and precious stones.

"Finally after returning by the luminous ladder to the earth, Mohammed untethered Boraq, mounted the saddle and rode into Jerusalem on the winged steed." The life of Mahomet, New York: pp 132-135).

Such is the report of the orientalist Dermenghem concerning the story of **al Isra'** and **al Mi'raj**. Every item he reported may be readily found, perhaps with greater or lesser detail, in many of the biographies. An example of the fertility of the resporters' imagination may be read in Ibn Hisham's biography. Reporting on Mohammed's conversation with Adam in the first heaven, Ibn-Hisham wrote:

"Then I saw men with lips like those of camels. In their hands were balls of fire which they thrusted into their mouths and collected from their extremities to thrust into their mouth again. I asked, `who are these, O Gabriel?' He said : `These are men who robbed the orphans.' I then saw a man with large bellies, the likes of which I have never seen before even on the road to the house of Pharaoh where the greatest punishment is meted out to the greatest sinners. These are trodden upon by men who when brought to the fire run like maddened camels. Those whom they treaded upon remain immobile, unable to move from their place. I asked, "Who are those, O Gabriel?'" He answered, `those are the usurers.' I then saw men sitting at a table loaded with delicious and fat meat as well as spoiled and stinking meat. They were eating of the latter and leaving the former untouched. I asked, `Who are these, O Gabriel?' He answered, `These are men who left their own women whom God permitted them to enjoy and ran after other women illegitimately! I then saw women hanging from their breasts and asked, `Who are these, O Gabriel?' He answered, `These are women who fathered on their husbands children not their own'.........He then took me into paradise where I saw a beautiful damsel with luscious lips. As I was attracted by her, I asked her, `To whom do you belong?' She answered, `To Zayd ibn Harithah'. The prophet of God (peace and blessings of Allah be upon him) announced this glad tiding to Zayd ibn Harithah."

Teaching Wudu and Prayer

Zayd bin Harithah is reported to have said that the Messenger of Allah (peace and blessings of Allah be upon him) said:

"Jibril came to me at the beginning of what he revealed to me and taught me how to do **Wudu** and the prayer....." (Ahmad in his *Musnad* and al-Hakam in his *Mustadrak*).

The Mesenger of Allah (peace and blessings of Allah be upon him) is reported to have said:

"Jibril descended and led me in the prayer and I prayed with him, then I prayed with him, then I prayed with him and then

I prayed with him", and he counted out five times on his
fingers." *(Al-Bukhari)*

Angels Coining Metaphor

Jabir bin `Abdullah is reported to have said:

"The angels came to the Prophet of Allah (peace and
blessings of Allah be upon him), while he was asleep and
some of them said, `He is asleep', while others said, `The eye
sleeps but the hearts awake'. They said, `There is a meta-
phor suitable for this companion of yours,' one said, `so coin'
a metaphor for him.' Some of them said, `He is asleep' and
others said, `The eye sleeps but the heart is awake.' They
said, `His metaphor is that of a man who builds a house and
lays out a feast in it and sends out a summoner to invite
people to it. All who answer the summoner enter the house
and partake of the feast. Those who do not answer the
summoner, do not enter the house and do not partake of the
feast'. They said, `Interpret it for him so that he can
understand it'. Some of them said, `He is asleep', and others
said, `The eye sleeps but the heart is awake'. They said, `The
house is the Garden and the caller is Mohammed (peace and
blessings of Allah be upon him). All who obey Mohammed
(peace and blessings of Allah be upon him), have obeyed
Allah. Those who disobey Mohammed (peace and blessings of Allah be upon him) have disobeyed Allah."
(Al-Bukhari).

Garden to Khadija

Abu Hurayra (may Allah be pleased with him) is reported to
have narrated:

"Jibril came to the Prophet of Allah (peace and blessings of Allah be upon him) and said:

"O Messenger of Allah, this is Khadija who is bringing with her a vessel containing condiments or food and drink. When she comes to you, greet her from her Lord and from me, and give her the good news of a house in the Garden made from a hollow pearl in which there will never be any shouting or tiredness."

At-Tibrani transmitted in *al-Awsat* from the **hadith** of Fatima (may Allah be pleased with her), who said:

`I said `Messenger of Allah, where is my mother Khadija? He said, `In a house made of hollow pearl.

`I said, `Where is the pearl?' "It is not like the kind of pearls which are strung as pearls and rubies."

As-Suhayli said, "The purpose of using the word **qasab** for pearl and not the word **lu'lu** is that there is inaptness in the word **qasab** since she carried the day `**ahrazat qasab assabaq**' by hastening to belief before anyone else.

He also said, "The mention of the house has a subtle meaning because she was the mistress of a house before the mission and then became the mistress of a house in Islam when there was no other house than hers, for there was no house of Islam on the face of the earth on the day when the Prophet of Allah (peace and blessings of Allah be upon him) was first sent except her house. It is a virtue which no one but she shares."

Ibn Hajar said:

"There is another meaning in the mention of the house because the people of the house of the Prophet of Allah (peace and blessings of Allah be upon him) derive it "

In the words, "any shouting or tiredless", **sakhab** means shouting and argumentation in which voices are raised, and **nasab** means exhaustion. As-Suhayli said that these two qualities, i.e. argumentation and fatigue, are apt because when the Prophet of Allah (peace and blessings of Allah be upon him) called people to Islam, Khadija (may Allah be pleased with her) answered him willingly and did not make him raise his voice nor quarrel nor tire in doing it. On the contrary she removed every fatigue from him and comforted him in every desolation and made every difficulty easy for him. Therefore it is fitting that the place which she was given the good news of by her Lord should have attirbute corresponding to her actions

After his words, "Greet her from her Lord and from me", *at-Tibrani* adds in his mission that she said. "He is peace and peace is from Him and peace be upon Jibril." In the variant of *an-Nasa'i*, she said, "Allah is peace and peace be upon Jibril and on you, O Messenger of Allah (peace and blessings of Allah be upon him).

Scholars say that this story contains an indication of Khadija's superior understanding because she did not say, "And upon you be peace", as was the case with some of the Companions when they used to say in the *Tashahhud,* "peace be upon Allah". The Prophet of Allah (peace and blessings of Allah be upon him) forbade them saying, "Allah is peace", so say: "Greetings belong to Allah." Thus Khadija, by the soundness of her understanding knows that Allah does not have the word "peace" in the reply to Him as creatures do because peace (*salam*) is one of the Names of Allah, and He also is called *Salawa*, and neither of them are correct to he used in replying to Allah.

In the Battle of Badr

Allah Almighty says:

وَلَقَدْ نَصَرَكُمُ اللّهُ بِبَدْرٍ وَأَنْتُمْ
أَذِلَّةٌ فَاتَّقُوا اللّهَ لَعَلَّكُمْ تَشْكُرُونَ ۞ إِذْ تَقُولُ لِلْمُؤْمِنِينَ
أَلَنْ يَكْفِيَكُمْ أَنْ يُمِدَّكُمْ رَبُّكُمْ بِثَلَاثَةِ آلَافٍ مِنَ الْمَلَائِكَةِ
مُنْزَلِينَ ۞ بَلَى إِنْ تَصْبِرُوا وَتَتَّقُوا وَيَأْتُوكُمْ مِنْ فَوْرِهِمْ
هَذَا يُمْدِدْكُمْ رَبُّكُمْ بِخَمْسَةِ آلَافٍ مِنَ الْمَلَائِكَةِ مُسَوِّمِينَ ۞
وَمَا جَعَلَهُ اللّهُ إِلَّا بُشْرَى لَكُمْ وَلِتَطْمَئِنَّ قُلُوبُكُمْ بِهِ وَمَا
النَّصْرُ إِلَّا مِنْ عِنْدِ اللّهِ الْعَزِيزِ الْحَكِيمِ ۞

"And Allah most surely helped you at Badr when you were
utterly weak. So fear Allah that you may be really grateful (to
Him). (Recall) when you said to the believers: Is it not
enough that your Lord should reinforce you with three
thousand Angels sent down? Yea if you are patient and
God-fearing, and the enemy should fall upon you all of a
sudden, your Lord shall reinforce you with five thousand
Angels attacking vehemently. And Allah made not that but
as a glad tiding for you and your hearts should thereby be set
at rest---and no succour is there but from Allah, the Mighty,
the Wise.   (Q. 3:123-126).

And He says in Sura al-Anfal:

إِذْ يُوحِي رَبُّكَ إِلَى الْمَلَائِكَةِ أَنِّي مَعَكُمْ فَثَبِّتُوا الَّذِينَ آمَنُوا
سَأُلْقِي فِي قُلُوبِ الَّذِينَ كَفَرُوا الرُّعْبَ فَاضْرِبُوا فَوْقَ
الْأَعْنَاقِ وَاضْرِبُوا مِنْهُمْ كُلَّ بَنَانٍ

"Remember thy Lord inspired the Angels (with the message); I am with you : give firmness to the Believers : I will
instil terror into the hearts of the unbelievers : Smite ye above

their necks and mite all their finger-tips off them". (Q. 8:12)

Badr is a camping ground and market, about twenty miles south-west of Madina noted for plentiful supply of water and situated at the union of the road from Madina and caravan route of Syria to Makkah. In respect of numerical strength and equipment the Muslims were no match for the Makkans, but they had implicit faith in the help and power of the Lord, and it was with his help that the band of the Muslims consisting of 313 men, hastily recruited and ill-equipped, gave crushing defeat to the Makkan's army which consisted of more than one thousand fighters, all well-equipped and well-trained. The battle was fought on the 17th of Ramadhan in the 2 Hijra (11th of March 624 A.D.).

A question arises in the mind of the people why is it that in Surah Anfal, the strength of the angels who came for help of the Muslims is described as one thousand, while here it is described as three thousands. The reason for the variation is that the actual strength was one thousand as was the number of the soldiers of the Makkan army. Here in Surah `Aal-e-Imran' amidst the battle at Badr a news was afloat that Kurz bin Jabir al-Maharbi was coming with a reinforcement for helping the Makkans. The Muslims felt perturbed. It was at this juncture that the Holy Prophet was promised by Allah that he and His men would be aided by more angels. As Kurz did not come, so the angels were not sent down.

Here the strength of the angels described is five thousand which is conditional with two things : If the Muslims are patient and God-fearing and they are attacked all of a sudden. As there was no sudden attack upon them, so Allah sent this revelation to strengthen their hearts.

One lesson of the Battle of Badr for the Believers is that whatever happens, whether there is a miracle or not, all help proceeds from Allah. Man should not be so arrogant as to suppose that his own resources will change the current of the world plan. Allah helps those who show constancy, courage, and discipline and use all the human means at their disposal, not those who fold their hands and have no faith. But Allah's help is determined on considerations exalted far above our petty human motives, and by perfect wisdom, of which we can have only faint glimpses.

The Angels are the troops of Allah. He strikes with them any of His slaves He wishes. Allah Almighty informs us that He helped the Muslims in the Battle of Badr by means of the Angels in answer to their call for help and to strengthen them with the supporst and feeling of tranquility that the angels cast into their hearts.

Ar-Rabi bin Anas said : "Allah helped the Muslims with a thousand and then they became 3000 and then 5000."

Al-Bukhari says in his **Sahih** in the "Chapter of the Presence of the Angels at Badr" from Mu'adh bin Rifa'a bin Rafi az-Zurqi from his father who was one of the people of Badr. He said:

"Jibril came to the Prophet of Allah (peace and blessings of Allah be upon him) and said : `How do you guage the people of Badr among you?' He said, `Among the best of the Muslims'. He said, `It is the same with those of the Angels who were present at Badr'."

Ar-Rabi bin Anas said:
"On the day of Badr people could see those who had been slain by the Angels among the dead by the blows above the necks and on their finger tips which looked as if fire had burnt them." (*Al-Baihiqi* transmitted it).
Al-Qurtubi said:

"The descent of the angels is one of the means of achieving victory which is in itself not necessary for the Almighty Lord but which His creatures do need. Therefore the heart should be connected to Allah and have trust in Him, for He is the One who helps both through means and also without means, "His command when He desires something is but to say to it, `Be!' and it is." (Q. 36:81). That does not diminish trust in Allah in any way and it refutes those who say that means are only for the weak, not the strong. The Prophet of Allah (peace and blessings of Allah be upon him) and his Companions were the strong and other people are the weak. This is clear."

The Battle of the Trench

Allah Almighty says:

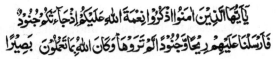

"O ye who believe! Remember of the Grace of Allah, (bestowed) on you, when there came down on you hosts (to overwhelm you) : but We sent against them a hurricane and forces that ye saw not : but Allah sees (clearly) all that ye do."
(Q. 33:9)

In this verse is summed up the beginning and the end of the fateful struggle of the Siege of Madinah in A.H. 5. The composition of the unhollowed confederacy that came to destroy Islam is referred to in the Introduction. They came with a forc of ten to twelve thousand fighting men, an unprecedented army for that time and country. The battle is known as the Battle of Trench.

After a close investment of two to four weeks, during which the enemy were disheartened by their futile siege, there was a peircing blast of the cold east wind. It was a severe winter, February can be a very cold month in Madinah, which is about

3,000 ft. above the sea-level. The enemy's tents were torn up, their fires were extinguished, the sand and rain beat in their faces, and they were terrified by the pertinents against them. They had already well nigh fallen out amongst themselves, and beating a hasty retreat, they melted away. The Madinah fighting strength was no more than 3,000 and the Jewish tribe of the Banu Quraiza who were in their midst was a source of weakness as they were treacherously intriguing with the enemy. And further there were the Hypocrites. But there were hidden forces that helped the Muslims. Besides the forces of nature there were Angels, though invisible to them, who assisted the Muslims.

Allah Almighty sees everything. Therefore we may conclude that the discipline and moral fervour of the Muslims, as well as the enmy's insincerities, intrigues, and reliance on brute force, were all contributory causes to the repulse, under Allah's dispensation. There were many hidden causes which neither party saw clearly.

Ibn Kathir says that the Almighty reports about His blessings, bounty and goodness to His believing slaves in averting there enemies and defeating them in the year in which they joined forces and allied themselves against them. That is referring to the Affair of the Ditch which took place in Shawwal, 5 A.H., according to most well-known sources.

Musa bin `Uqba and others said that it happened in 4 A.H., and that the reascn the Confederates came was that a group of Jewish nobles of Banu'-Nadir, who had been exiled from Madinah by the Messenger of Allah to Khaybar, including Sallam bin Abi'l-Huqaq, went to Makkah and met with the nobles of Quraysh and encouraged them to attack the Prophet of Allah (peace and blessings of Allah be upon him), promising them their help and support. They agreed to do it.

Then they went out to the tribe of Ghatafan and invited them, and they also agreed. Quraysh went out with their battalions followig them led by Abu Sufyan, Sakhr bin Harb. Incharge of Ghatafan was Yayna bin Hisn Hudhayfa. Altogether they numbered about 10,000 men.

When the Messenger of Allah (peace and blessings of Allah be upon him) learned of their advance, he commanded the Muslims to dig a ditch around Madinah on the eastern side. That was on the suggestion of Salman al-Farisi (may Allah be pleased with him). So the Muslims worked on it, putting much effort into it and the Messenger of Allah (peace and blessings of Allah be upon him) shifted the earth and dug with them.

The idol worshippers came and camped on the eastern side of the city near Uhud and another group of them camped in the upper part of Madinah as the Almighty says. **"When they came at you from above you and below you."**

The Messenger of Allah (peace and blessings of Allah be upon him) and the Muslims with him came out. There were about 3,000 of them though some say 7,000. They had their backs to Sal' and their faces towards the enemy. The ditch had been dug, but there was no water in it to stop the horses and men from reaching them. He kept the women and children inside the fortress of Madinah.

The Banu Qurayza were a tribe of Jews who had fortress to the east of Madinah and they had a treaty with Prophet of Allah (peace and blessings of Allah be upon him). They had abut 800 fighters. Huyayy of the Banu Nadir went to them and kept at them until they broke their treaty and supported the confederates against the Messenger of Allah (peace and blessings of Allah be upon him). Thus the danger was great, the business very grave and the situation dire as Allah Almighty says, **"At that time the believers were tested and severely shaken."**

They continued to besiege the Prophet of Allah (peace and blessings of Allah be upon him) and his Companions for about a month although they did not attack them and there was no fighting between them except when `Amir bin `Abdu Wudd al-Amiri, one of the bold horsemen famous in the **Jahiliyya**, rode forward with some horsemen and crossed the ditch, reaching part of the Muslims. The Messenger of Allah (peace and blessings of Allah be upon him) detailed some riders of the Muslim to face him. It is also said that no one went out to him. He commanded Ali (may Allah be pleased with him) to out do him and they fought for some time and then Ali killed him. That was a sign of impending victory.

Then Allah Almighty sent a strong wind against the Confederates which blew so fiercely that they had no tents left standing nor could they light a fire nor would anything stay in its place. So they left in disappointment and loss as the Almighty says:

يَـٰٓأَيُّهَا ٱلَّذِينَ ءَامَنُواْ ٱذْكُرُواْ نِعْمَةَ ٱللَّهِ عَلَيْكُمْ إِذْ جَآءَتْكُمْ جُنُودٌ
فَأَرْسَلْنَا عَلَيْهِمْ رِيحًا وَجُنُودًا لَّمْ تَرَوْهَا وَكَانَ ٱللَّهُ بِمَا تَعْمَلُونَ بَصِيرًا

"O you who believe! Remember Allah's blessings to you when forces came against you and We sent against them a wind and other forces that you could not see." (Q. 33:9)

Ibn Kathir says that His words, "other forces you could not see", mean the Angels who unsettled them and cast terror and fear into their hearts. The leader of every tribe said, "O Banu so-and so! To me!" and they gathered to him and he was saying "Help!" When Allah Almighty cast terror in their hearts.

Action against Bani Qurayza

Not long after his arrival in Madinah, the Prophet of Allah (peace and blessings of Allah be upon him) got a covenant made between *Ansar* and *Muhajirin* to which the Jews were also made a party and guaranteed protection of life and property as well as freedom of professing their faith. The covenant, which was reduced to writing accepted certain rights of the Jews and also put them under certain obligations. Some of the important clauses of this covenant were as follows:

> "Those among the Jews who side with us shall be liable to equality and help. Neither shall they be wronged nor shall their enemies be given any help. No polytheist of Madinah shall afford protection. to the property or life of any Qurayshite, nor shall he intervene against a believer on their behalf. The Jews shall bear the expenses of war, so long as the war lasts, like the believers, the Jews shall be considered as one community alongwith the believers -- they shall have the freedom of their religion and the believers shall be free to profess their faith. They shall have full freedom with their allies and slaves and to settle their affairs."

The covenant also made both the parties liable to help one another in the event of war, and, subject to the limits of divine injuctions, to promote mutual co-operation, goodwill and cordial relations between the confederates. One of its clauses provided that if Yathrib was attacked by an enemy, both the Jews and the Muslims shall join hands in its defence.

(*Ibn Hisham*, vol. II, pp. 503-4).

But inspite of these clear undertakings, Bani Qurayza were won over by Huyayy bin Akhtab al-Nadir to go back on their words in order to help the Quraysh. As a matter of fact, when Huyayy bin Akhtab had come to Bani Qurayza for winning them over to the allies against the Muslims, their chief K'ab bin Asad had replied, "I have always found Mohammed (peace and blessings of Allah be upon him) truthful and trustworthy." However, K'ab bin Asad broke his word and absolved himself of every responsibility devolving upon him by the covenant.

When the Prophet of Allah (peace and blessings of Allah be upon him) heard of the betrayal of Bani Qurayza, he deputed a few persons including S'ad bin Mu'adh and S'ad bin Ubada, the two chiefs of Aus and Khazraj, to see if the report was correct. They found out that the situation was even worse than they had heard. Bani Qurayza spoke disparagingly of the Apostle and said, "Who is the apostle of God? We have no pact or pledge with Mohammed (peace and blessings of Allah be upon him).

Bani Qurayza then started making preparation for an armed conflict with the Muslims; they threatened to stab in the back and actually placed the Apostle and his followers between the hammer and the anvil. Actually the situation would not have been so hazardous had the Jews declared their intention, in the very beginning to fall out of the Muslims. The plight of the Muslims has been depicted picturesquely by the Qur'an:

$$ إِذْ جَآءُوكُمْ مِّن فَوْقِكُمْ وَمِنْ أَسْفَلَ مِنكُمْ وَإِذْ زَاغَتِ الْأَبْصَارُ وَبَلَغَتِ الْقُلُوبُ الْحَنَاجِرَ وَتَظُنُّونَ بِاللّٰهِ الظُّنُونَا ﴿ $$

"When they came upon you from above you and from below you?" (Q. 33:10).

It was but natural that the Muslims fet hurt by the perfidy of the Jews. How hard had it striken the Muslims can be judged from the prayer sent up fervently by S`ad bin Mu`adh the chief of Aus. He had been in partnership with these Jews for many years and was, thus, their ally and sympathizer. When he was shot by an arrow which severed the vein of his arm and he lost the hope of surviving for long, he supplicated to Allah, saying:

"O Allah do not let me die until I have set my eyes on the destruction of Bani Qurayza."

The Prophet of Allah (peace and blessings of Allah be upon him) as well as the Muslims laid their arms aside on return from the Battle of Trench. On account of what happened thereafter, as related by the Traditions, is that Jibril came to the Prophet and asked, "O Apostle of Allah, have you put aside your arms?" When the Apostle replied that he had, Jibril said, "But the Angels have not put away their arms. "Allah commands you", continued Jibril, "to march on Bani Qurayza. I am also to go there to flutter them. "Thereupon the Prophet got an announcement made that every one who listened and followed him ought to perform the Asr prayer at Bani Qurayza.

The Prophet besieged the district inhabited by the Jewish clan of Bani Qurayza. The beleagured Jews defied the seige for twenty-five days after which they gave in and offered to surrender. Allah cast terror into their hearts.

Bukhari reports from Anas bin Malik (may Allah be pleased with him):

"It is as if I could see the dust rising in the valley of the Bani Ghanm from the procession of Jibril when the Messenger of Allah (peace and blessings of Allah be upon him) went to Banu Qurayza.

Musa bin Uqba said narrated from az-Zuhri, "Jibril said to the Prophet of Allah (peace and blessings of Allah be upon him), "May Allah forgive you! Have you laid down your weapons?" He said, 'Yes'. Jibril said, `We have not laid them down since the time the enemy first came upon you and I was seeking them out until Allah Almighty defeated them'. They say that traces of dust were on ʾibril's face. Jibril said to him, Allah commands you to fight Banu Qurayza and I am going to them with those of the Angels who are with me to shake their fortresses, so bring out the people.'

The Messenger of Allah (peace and blessings of Allah be upon him) went out after Jibril and passed by a gathering of Banu Ghanm who were waiting for the Messenger of Allah (peace and blessings of Allah be upon him) and he asked them. `Did a horseman just pass by you?' They replied, `Dihya al-Kalbi passed by us on a white horse with a brocade cloth or rug under him wearing a bandage'. They mentioned that the Messenger of Allah (peace and blessings of Allah be upon him) said, `that was Jibril'. The Messenger of Allah (peace and blessings of Allah be upon him) used to say that Dihya resembled Jibril.

Battle of Hunain

Allah Almighty says :

لَقَدْ نَصَرَكُمُ اللهُ فِي
مَوَاطِنَ كَثِيرَةٍ وَّيَوْمَ حُنَيْنٍ إِذْ أَعْجَبَتْكُمْ كَثْرَتُكُمْ
فَلَمْ تُغْنِ عَنْكُمْ شَيْئًا وَّضَاقَتْ عَلَيْكُمُ الْأَرْضُ بِمَا
رَحُبَتْ ثُمَّ وَلَّيْتُمْ مُّدْبِرِينَ ۞ ثُمَّ أَنْزَلَ اللهُ سَكِينَتَهُ
عَلَى رَسُولِهِ وَعَلَى الْمُؤْمِنِينَ وَأَنْزَلَ جُنُودًا لَّمْ تَرَوْهَا ،
وَعَذَّبَ الَّذِينَ كَفَرُوا ۗ وَذَلِكَ جَزَآءُ الْكَافِرِينَ ۞

"Assuredly Allah did help you in many battle-fields and on the day of Hunain : Behold! your numbers elated you, but they availed you naught; the land. for all that it is wide, did constrain you and ye turned back in retreat. But Allah did pour His calm on the Messenger and on the Believers, and sent down forces which ye saw not : He punished the Unbelievers, thus doth He reward those without Faith."

(Q. 9:25-26)

Hunain is on the road to Taif from Makkah about fourteen miles to the east of Makkah. It is a village in the mountainous country between Makkah and Taif. Immediately after the conquest of Makkah, (A.H.8), the Pagan idolators, who were surprised and chagrined at the wonderful reception which Islam was receiving, organised a great gathering near Taif to concert plans for attacking the Prophet. The Hawazin and the Thaqif tribes took the lead and prepared great expedition for Makkah, boasting of their strength and military skill. There was, on the other hand, a wave of confident enthusiasm among the Muslims at Makkah, in which the new Muslims joined. The enemy forces numbered about 4,000 but the Muslim forces reached a total of ten or twelve thousand, as every one wished to join. The battle was fought at Hunain.

For the first time the Muslims had at Hunain tremendous odds in their favour. But this itself constituted a danger. Many in the ranks had more enthusiasm than wisdom, more a spirit of elation than of faith and confidence in the righteousness of their cause. The enemy had the advantage of knowing the ground thoroughly. They laid an ambush in which the advance guard of the Muslim force was caught. The country is hilly, in which the enemy concealed himself. As soon as the Muslim vanguard entered the Hunain valley, the enemy fell upon them with fury and caused havoc with their arrows from their places of concealment. In such ground the number of the Muslims were themselves a disadvantage. Many were slain, and many turned back in confusion and retreated. But the Prophet, as ever, was calm in his wisdom and faith. He rallied his forces and inflicted the most crushing defeat on the enemy.

Sakina : calm, peace, security, tranquility. The Prophet of Allah (peace and blessings of Allah be upon him) never approved of over-weening confidence or reliance merely upon human strength, or human resources or numbers. In the hour of danger as seeming disaster, he was perfectly calm, and with cool courage relied upon the help of Allah. Whose standard he carried. His calmness inspired all around him, and stopped the rout of those who had turned their backs. It was with Allah's help that they won, and their victory was complete. They followed it up with an energetic pursuit of the enemies, capturing their camps, their flocks and herds, and their families, whom they had boastfully brought with them in expectation of an easy victory.

Ibn Kathir said, "The Almighty mentioned to the believers His bounty to them and His goodness to them in helping them on many occasions in their expeditions with His Messenger and that their success was from Him and by His support and determination not by reason of their numbers. He informed them that help is from Him whether the group is big or small. On the day of Hunain they admired their numbers but this did not help them in any way and they trued in retreat, all but a few of them who stayed with the Messenger of Allah (peace and blessings of Allah be upon him). Then Allah's help and His support descended on His Messenger and on the believers who were with him to teach them that victory is from the Almighty alone.

$$ كَمْ مِّن فِئَةٍ قَلِيلَةٍ غَلَبَتْ فِئَةً كَثِيرَةً بِإِذْنِ اللَّهِ وَاللَّهُ مَعَ الصَّابِرِينَ $$

Even if the group is small, how many a small force has truimphed over much greater numbers by the permission of Allah. Allah is with the steadfast."   (Q. 2:249)

It was the 10th of Shaw'wal, 8. A.H., when the Muslim army reached Hunain, descending the *Wadi* in morning twilight, the enemy had taken its position in the glens and hollows and creators of the valley. A volley of arrows was all that the Muslims saw of the enemy. Then suddenly the enemy followed up the attack with full force. Hawazin were celebrated archers.

The sudden onslaught forced the Muslim flanks to fall back

and they fled in terror none heeding the other. The battle had taken a dangerous turn; and complete rout of the Muslims was in sight without any possibility of an orderly retreat or rallying of their forces again. Like the Uhad when the rumour of the apostle's death had disheartened the Muslims, the troops were once more driven to despair in Hunain by a similar misgiving.

Some of the rude fellows from Makkah who had joined the Muslim army but were still not strong in faith started talking in a way that let out thier antipathy to Islam. One said, "their flight will not stop before they get at the sea." Another man remarked, "The spell of their sorcery had ended today."

The Muslims had to suffer this defeat after the brilliant victory of Makkah as if by way of punishment for their reliance on numbers instead of the succour of Allah. Their faith needed to be strengthened by a misadventure for they had to learn the lesson that both victory and defeat came from Allah; neither the one should make m an exultant nor despondent. The Muslims were all over with their trepidation when the peace of Allah appeared to be descending on them and to Apostle. The Prophet had all the while stood firm, riding his white mule, without any fear or fidgets. Only a few of the *Ansar* and *Muhajirin* or his relatives were then with him. Abbas bin Abdul Muttalib was holding the bridle of his mule while Allah's Apostle was calling aloud : "Verily, I am the Prophet without falsehood; I am son of Abdul Muttalib." (According to Bukhari, Abu Sufyan bin al-Harith was holding the bridle.)

In the mean time a detatchment of the enemy advanced towards him. The Prophet took a handful of dust and threw it into their eyes.

When the Prophet of Allah (peace and blessings of Allah be upon him) saw his men in confusion, he said, "O Abbas call out, `O Ansar, O Comrades of the acacia tree." All those who heard the cry, responded, "Here are we." Abbas has a loud voice. Whoever heard him calling got off from his camel and came to the Apostle. When sufficent number of men had gathered they bore down upon the enemy. A combat between the two parties started afresh. The Apostle then took to a height alongwith some of his Companions. He saw the two sides grappled with one another. He said, "Now the battle has grown hot." He threw a few pebbles on the enemy. ` Abbas relates that he saw the enemy becoming slack thereafter losing the day to the Muslims.

Both the armies fought bravely. However before all those Muslims who had fled away had come back, the enemy was discomfited and a party of handcuffed prisoners was brought before the Apostle. Allah helped the Apostle with the hosts of heaven to the day and brought Hawazin to their knees :

> "Allah hath given you victory on many battle-fields and on the day of Hunain, when ye exulted in your multitude but it availed you naught, and the earth, vast as it is, straightened for you; then ye turned back in flight;

> "Then Allah sent His peace of reassurance down upon His Messenger and upon the believers, and sent down hosts ye could not see, and punished those who disbelieved. Such is the reward of disbelievers"   (Q. 9:25-26)

The bitterness and rancour borne by the Pagans against Islam melted away after the Battle of Hunain. The last strong hold of paganism was toppled down in this battle and no formidable opponent of Islam remained in Arabia. The remaining tribes streamed to Madinah from every part of Arabia to put their trust in Allah and His Apostle.

Mika'il (Michael)

Mika'il (peace be upon him) is entrused with the rain and dispensing it whenever Allah Almighty commands him to. He possesses a high position, a lofty station and great honour with his Lord, the Almighty and Majestic. He has helpers who do everything he orders them to by the command of his Lord. They make the winds and clouds move as Allah, the Almighty and Exalted, wishes.

Ibn Abbas (may Allah be pleased with him) once asked Jibril (peace be upon him):
"What is Mika'il in charge of?"
"The plants and the rain." He replied *(Tibrani)*

Imam Ahmad reports from Anas bin Malik (may Allah be pleased with him) that the Prophet of Allah (peace and blessings of Allah be upon him) once asked Jibril (peace be upon him):

"Why do I never see Mika'il laugh?"

"Mika'il has not laughed since the Fire was created", He replied *(Musnad Ahmad)*.

Israfil

One among the main angels is Israfil (peace be upon him) who is entrusted with the trumpet. He will blow three blasts on it at the command of his lord, the Almighty and Exalted. The first is the Blast of Terror, the second the Blast of Swooning, and the third the Blast of the Rising for the Lord of heaven and earth.

Abu Sa'id al-Khudri (may Allah be pleased with him) said that the Messenger of Allah (peace and blessings of Allah be upon him) said:

"How can I enjoy myself when the one with the Trumpet has raised the trumpet to his mouth, knitted his brow and is waiting to blow."

"What should we say, Messenger of Allah?" they said. "Say: Allah is enough for us and the best Guardian. We have put our trust in Allah." he said.

These noble three----Jibril, Mika'il and Israfil (peace be upon them) are the leaders of the angels. The Messenger of Allah (peace and blessings of Allah be upon him) used to say in his supplication:

"O Allah, Lord of Jibril, Mika'il and Israfil, Bringer of the heavens and the earth into being, Knower of the unseen and visible, it is Thou who judges between Your slaves concerning the things about which they did. Guide us to the truth in respect of the things about which there is disagreement by Your permission. You guide whomever You will to a straight path."

Ibn al-Qayyim (may Allah have mercy on him), said:

"The Messenger of Allah (peace and blessings of Allah be upon him) pleaded with Allah Almighty by His overall Lordship and His particular Lordship over these three Angels who are the guardians of all life. Jibril is entrusted with the revelation by which hearts and souls are brought to life; Mika'il is entrusted with the rains by which land, plants and animals are brought to life; and Israfil is entrusted with the blowing by which all creatures will be brought to life after their death. Thereafter Allah's Messenger asked Allah by His Lordship over these Angels to guide him to the truth in respect of those things about which there is disagreement by His permission since in that lie all the benefits of life."

Izra'il (The Angel of Death)

One of the Angels is entrusted with the taking of the souls. He is the Angel of Death. Some reports call him Izra'il.

قُلْ يَتَوَفَّاكُمْ مَّلَكُ الْمَوْتِ الَّذِى وُكِّلَ بِكُمْ ثُمَّ إِلَى رَبِّكُمْ تُرْجَعُونَ

"Say: "The Angel of Death, put in charge of you, will (duly) take your souls : then shall ye be brought back to your Lord."
(Q. 32:11)

That is, if death is certain, as it is, and this life by itself in no way satisfies our instincts and expectations, we may be sure that the agency which separates our soul from our body will bring us into the new world. If we believe in a soul at all---the very foundation of Religion---we must believe in a Future, without which the soul has no meaning.

The Hypocrites believed in double dealing. Thus they came to the assemblies of Islam in Madinah and pretended to listen to the Prophet's teaching and preaching. But their heart and mind were not in learning righteousness, but in carping at thigs they saw and heard. When they got out, they knew nothing of the teachings, but on the contrary asked foolish and ignorant questions, such as might raise doubts. This hypocrisy is a disease. This is in fact, disloyalty to the Cause, want of courage and of the spirit of self-sacrifice, want of true understanding. Such men are crushed by Allah and they are deprived of His Grace and He left them straying, because they deliberately rejected His guidance. The result is that what they hear is as if they had not heard, and what they see is as if they had not seen. They have not desired to understand Allah's will or Allah's Revelation; or is it that they have themselves locked and bolted their hearts and minds, so that nothing can penetrate them?

Such men are entirely in the hands of Satan. They follow his suggestions, and their hopes are built on his deceptions. They have become so impervious to facts and truths, because, without the courage to oppose Allah's Cause openly, they secretly intrigue with Allah's enemies, and say that they will follow them part of the way, and be remaining partly in the other camp, they will be far more useful as spies and half-hearted-doubters than by going over altogether. If they think that this game will be successful, they are mistaken. All the inner secrets and motives of their hearts are known to Allah.

Allah Almighty says about the hypocrites :

فَكَيْفَ إِذَا تَوَفَّتْهُمُ الْمَلَٰئِكَةُ يَضْرِبُونَ وُجُوهَهُمْ وَأَدْبَارَهُمْ

"But how (will it be) when the Angels take their souls at death and smite their faces and their backs?"   (Q. 47:27)

It is all very well for them to practise hypocrisy in this life. How will they feel at death, when they find that the Angels know all, and touch the very spots they had taken such care to conceal?

Their faces and their backs : There is a subtle metaphor. The **face** is what looks to the front, the side you present to the outer world; the **back** is what is not shown, what is hidden from the world. The hypocrites will be hit at both points. Or the **face** is what boast of, what they are proud of, the **back** is the skeleton in the cupboard, the things they dare not utter, but which yet haunt them The hypocrites are hit on every side.

And Allah Almighty says about the believers :

الَّذِينَ تَتَوَفَّاهُمُ الْمَلَٰئِكَةُ طَيِّبِينَ يَقُولُونَ سَلَٰمٌ عَلَيْكُمُ ادْخُلُوا الْجَنَّةَ بِمَا كُنْتُمْ تَعْمَلُونَ

"(Namely) those whose lives the angels take in a state of purity, saying (to them), "peace be on you; enter ye the Garden, because of (the good) which ye did (in the world).
(Q. 16:32)

In a state of purity : from the evils of this world, from want of faith and want of grace. Purity from such evil is the mark of true Islam, and those who die in such purity will be received into Felicity with a salutation of Peace.

It has come in sound *hadiths* that the helpers of this Angel come to the dying person according to his actions. If he is a good-doer, then they have the best appearance and most beautiful form and bring the greatest good news. If he is evil, then they take on the ugliest appearance and most atrocious aspect and bear the harshest threat. Then they draw out the soul (until it reaches the dying person's throat where the Angel (of Death) takes it. They do not leave it in his hands, but wrap it in shrouds on the appropriate perfume. As the Almighty says":

فَلَوْلَا إِذَا بَلَغَتِ الْحُلْقُومَ ۞ وَأَنْتُمْ حِينَئِذٍ تَنْظُرُونَ ۞ وَنَحْنُ أَقْرَبُ إِلَيْهِ مِنْكُمْ وَلَكِنْ لَا تُبْصِرُونَ ۞ فَلَوْلَا إِنْ كُنْتُمْ غَيْرَ مَدِينِينَ ۞ تَرْجِعُونَهَا إِنْ كُنْتُمْ صَادِقِينَ ۞ فَأَمَّا إِنْ كَانَ مِنَ الْمُقَرَّبِينَ ۞ فَرَوْحٌ وَرَيْحَانٌ وَجَنَّتُ نَعِيمٍ ۞ وَأَمَّا إِنْ كَانَ مِنْ أَصْحَابِ الْيَمِينِ ۞ فَسَلَامٌ لَكَ مِنْ أَصْحَابِ الْيَمِينِ ۞ وَأَمَّا إِنْ كَانَ مِنَ الْمُكَذِّبِينَ الضَّالِّينَ ۞ فَنُزُلٌ مِنْ حَمِيمٍ ۞ وَتَصْلِيَةُ جَحِيمٍ ۞ إِنَّ هَذَا لَهُوَ حَقُّ الْيَقِينِ ۞ فَسَبِّحْ بِاسْمِ رَبِّكَ الْعَظِيمِ ۞

"Then why do ye not (intervene) when (the soul of the dying man) reaches the throat. And ye the while (sit) looking on,-

but We are nearer to him than ye, and yet see not,--then why do ye not, --if ye are true (in your claim of independence)? Thus, then, if he be of those Nearest to Allah, (there is for him) Rest and Satisfaction and a Garden of Delights; And if he be of the Companions of the Right Hand, (for him is the salutaion), "peace be unto thee", from the Companions of the Right Hand. And if he be of those who deny (the truth) who go wrong, for him is Entertainment with Boiling Water and burning in Hell-Fire. Verily this is the very Truth of assured Certainty. So glorify the name of the Lord, the Supreme."   (Q. 56:83-96)

The dying man's friends, relatives and companions may be sitting round him and quite close to him in his last moments, but Allah is nearer still at all times, for He is nearer than the man's own jugular vein.

The sentence may now be briefly paraphrased, `If you disbelieve in Revelation and a future Judgement, and claim to do what you like and be independent of Allah, how is it you cannot call back a dying man's soul to his body when all of you congregate round him at his death bed? But you are not independent of Judgement. There is a Day of Account, when you will have to be judged by your deeds in this life.'

Another type of angels are those entrusted with guardianship of each person both at home and while travelling, in his sleep and when awake, and in all his states. They are those who take over from one another. Allah Almighty says:

"It is the same (to Him) whether any of you conceals his speech or declares it openly; whether he lies hidden by night or walks freely by the day. For each (such person) there are (angels) in succession, before and behind him; they guard him by command of Allah. Verily never will Allah change the condition of a people until they change what is in themselves but when (once) Allah willeth a people's punishment, there can be no turning it back, nor will they find, besides Him, any to protect"   (Q.13:10-11)

Every person, whether he conceals or reveals his thoughts, whether he sulks in darkness or goes about by day, --all are under Allah's watch and ward. His Grace encompasses everyone, and again and again protects him, if he will only take the protection, from harm and evil. If in his folly he thinks he can secretly take some pleasure or profit, he is wrong, for recording angels record all his thoughts and deeds.

Allah Almighty is not intent on punishment. He created man virtuous and pure: He gave him intelligence and knowledge. He surrounded him will all sorts of instruments of His grace and mercy. If, in spite of all this man distorts his own will and goes against Allah's Will, yet is Allah's forgiveness open to him if he will take it. It is only when he has made his own sight blind and changed his own nature or soul away from the beautiful mould in which Allah formed it, Allah's Wrath will descend on him and the favourable position in which Allah placed him will be changed. When once the punishment comes, there is no turning it back. None of the things which he relied upon---other than Allah--can possibly protect him Allah Almighty says :

وَهُوَالْقَاهِرُ فَوْقَ عِبَادِهِ وَيُرْسِلُ عَلَيْكُمْ حَفَظَةً حَتَّى إِذَا جَاءَ أَحَدَكُمُ الْمَوْتُ تَوَفَّتْهُ رُسُلُنَا وَهُمْ لَا يُفَرِّطُونَ

"He is irresistible, supreme over His servants and He sets guardians over you. At length, when death approaches one of you Our Angels take his soul and they never fail in their duty."   (Q. 6:61).

Most commentators understand this to mean "guardian angels". The idea of guardianship is expressed in a general term. Allah Almighty watches over us and guards us and provides all kinds of agencies, material, and spiritual, to help our growth and development, keep us from harm, and bring us near to our Destiny. When death approaches one of you Our angels take his soul, and they never fail in their duty.

Here the word used is *rusul*, the Sent ones, the same word as for human Messengers sent by Allah to teach mankind. The angels who come to take out souls at death are accurate in the performance of their duty. They come neither before nor after their appointed time, nor do they do it in any manner other than that fixed by the Command of Allah.

Ibn Abbas (may Allah be pleased with him) says:

"The angels protect man in front and behind. When Allah's decree comes, they leave him."

Mujahid says:

"There is no one who does not have an angel who is entrusted with protecting him both when asleep and when awake, from jinn and men and reptiles. None of them comes to him without finding an angel blocking its way except for something which Allah has given permission to reach him."

Angels --- Right and Left

These angels are entrusted with preserving the record of each person's good and evil actions.

Allah Almighty says :

أَمْ يَحْسَبُونَ أَنَّا لَا نَسْمَعُ سِرَّهُمْ وَنَجْوَاهُمْ بَلَى وَرُسُلُنَا لَدَيْهِمْ
يَكْتُبُونَ

"Or do they think that We hear not their secrets and their
private counsels? Indeed (We do), and Our Messengers
are by them to record." (Q. 43:80)

However secretly men may plot, everything is known to Allah.
His Recording Angels are by, at all time and in all places, to prepare
a Record of their Deeds for their own conviction when the time
comes for judgement.

And He says :

مَايَلْفِظُ مِنْ قَوْلٍ إِلَّا لَدَيْهِ رَقِيبٌ عَتِيدٌ ۞ وَ جَآءَتْ سَكْرَةُ الْمَوْتِ بِالْحَقِّ
ذٰلِكَ مَاكُنْتَ مِنْهُ تَحِيدُ ۞ وَنُفِخَ فِى الصُّوْرِ ذٰلِكَ يَوْمُ الْوَعِيدِ ۞ وَجَآءَتْ كُلُّ
نَفْسٍ مَّعَهَا سَآئِقٌ وَّشَهِيدٌ

"Behold, two (guardian angels) appointed to learn (his
doing) learn (and note them), one sitting on the right and one
on the left. Not a word does he utter but there is a vigilant
Guardian. And the stupor of death comes in truth. This was
the thing which thou was trying to escape! And the Trumpet
shall be blown : that will be the Day whereof Warning (had
been given). And there will come forth every soul : with each
will be an (angel) to drive, and an (angel) to bear witness."
(Q. 50:17-21)

That is, two angels are constantly by him to note his thoughts,
words, and actions. One sits on the right side and notes his good
deeds and the other on the left, to note his bad deeds; corresponding to the Companion of the Right and the Companion of the Left.

The each 'word' spoken is taken down by a guardian (raqib).
This has been construed to mean that the guardian only records
words not thoughts which are not uttered. Thoughts may be
forgiven if not uttered, and still more if they do not issue in action.

At the stage at which we clothe a thought in words, we have already done an action. The Recorders mentioned in the last verse make a complete Record, in order to supply motives and springs of action, which will affect the degree or a status in the Hereafter. The three together, individuals or kinds, make the honourable Recorders, *Kiraman Katibin.*

What is stupor or unconsciousness to this probationary life will be the opening of the eyes to the next world : for Death is the Gateway between the two. Once through that Gateway man will realise how the things which he neglected or looked upon as remote are the intimate Realities, and the things he wanted to avoid are the things that have really come to pass. Both Good and Evil will realise the Truth now in its intensity.

The next stage will be the Judgement, heralded with the blowing of the Trumpet. Every soul will then come forth.

Here several interpretations are possible, leading to the same truth, that the Judgement will be set up; the Record will be produced, the good and bad deeds will speak for and against and complete justice will be done, each act leading to its own due fruit

(1) (angels) to drive and the (angel) to bear witness may be the Recording angels of the left and the right; or

(2) it may not be angels, but the evil deeds will drive like task-masters, and the good deeds will bear witness for the soul on trial;

(3) his misused limbs and faculties will drive him to his doom, while his well-used limbs and faculties will witness for him.

Allah Almighty says ·

وَإِنَّ عَلَيْكُمْ لَحَفِظِيْنَ ۝ كِرَامًا كَاتِبِيْنَ ۝ يَعْلَمُوْنَ مَا تَفْعَلُوْنَ ۝

"But verily over you (are appointed angels) to protect you,
--kind and honourable, --writing down (your deeds) : they
know all that ye do."   (Q. 82:10-12)

Besides the faculties given to man to guide him, and the Form
and Personality through which he can rise by stages to the
Presence of Allah, there are spiritual agencies around him
to help and protect him, and to note down his Record, so
that perfect justice may be done to him at the end.

Ibn Abi Hatim transmits with his *isnad* from Mujahid that the
Messenger of Allah (peace and blessings of Allah be upon him)
said:

> "Honour the noble scribes who only leave you at two times
> : in *Janaba* and when you relieve yourselves. When one of
> you has a *ghusl*, he should screen himself with a wall or his
> camel, or his brother should screen him."

Sufyan was asked, "How do the angels know the person
intends a good or evil action?" He replied, "When someone intends
a good action, they smell the scent of musk coming from him, and
when he intends an evil action, they smell a putrid smell coming from
him. Al-Bukhari transmitted with his *isnad* from Abu Hurairah
(may Allah be pleased with him) that the Messenger of Allah
(peace and blessings of Allah be upon him) said:

> "Allah Almighty has said, `When My slave wants to do an
> evil action, you should not write it down until he does it. If
> he does it, then write down the equivalent of it. If he does
> not do it for My sake, then write it down as a good action
> for him. If he wants to do a good action and does not do it,
> then write down as a good action. If he does do it then write
> down ten to seven hundred of its like."

Ibn Hajr said in a*l-Fath*, "This *hadith* indicates that the angel is aware of what is in the heart of the human being, either by Allah acquainting him with it or by creating for him knowledge by which he percieves it."

Al-Hasan al-Basri said about the *ayah* :

إِذْ يَتَلَقَّى الْمُتَلَقِّيَانِ عَنِ الْيَمِينِ وَعَنِ الشِّمَالِ قَعِيدٌ

"Behold, two (guardian angels) appointed to learn (his doings) learn (and note them), one sitting on the right and one one the left."   (Q. 50:17)

"O' Son of Adam! A scroll has been unfurled for you and two noble angels have been entrusted with you, one on your right and the other on your left. The one on your right records your good actions. The one on your left records your evil actions. So do what you wish, whether it is a little or a lot. Then, when you die, your scroll will be rolled up and placed by your neck with you in your grave until you emerge on the Day of Rising. Then Allah Almighty will say : "Every man's fate We have fastened on his own neck : on the Day of Judgement We shall bring out for him a scroll, which he will see spread open. (It will be said to him:) "Read thine (own) record : Sufficient is thy soul this day to make out an account against thee."

Fate: **Tair**, literally a bird, hence an omen, an evil fate. The Arabs, the ancient Romans, sought to read the mysteries of human fate from the flight of birds. And many of us in our own day seek to read our future fortunes by similar superstitions. We read in the previous verse that there are Signs of Allah, but they are not meant to subserve the vulgar purpose of disclosing our future destiny in a worldly sense. They are meant to subserve the vulgar purpose of disclosing our destiny in a worldly sense. They are meant to quite other purposes, as we have explained. Our real fate does not depend upon birds or omens or stars. It depends on our deeds; good or evil, and they hang round our necks.

These deeds, good or evil, will be embodied in a scroll which will be quite open to us in the light of Day of Judgement, however much we may affect to be ignorant of it now or waste our energies in prying into mysteries that do not concern us.

Our true accusers are our own deeds. Why not look to them instead of vanity prying into something superstitious which we call a book of future or a book of omens?

Al-Bukhari transmitted with his *isnad* from Abu Hurairah (may Allah be pleased with him) that the Messenger of Allah (peace and blessings of Allah be upon him) said:

> "The angels of the night and the angels of the day take turns in attending you and they meet at the `Asr' prayer and the Fajr prayer. Then those who spent the night with you ascend and He questions them, although He knows better than them. He says, `How did you leave My slaves?" They say, `We left them which they were praying and we came to them while they were praying."

He also transmitted from Abu Musa (may Allah be pleased with him) who said:

> "The Messengers of Allah (peace and blessings of Allah be upon him) stood up in our midst and made four statements. He said, `Allah does not sleep and it is not proper for Him to sleep; He lessens and increases what is alloted to you; the actions of the night are presented to Him before the actions of the day; and actions of the day are presented to Him before the action of the night.

Munkar and Nakir

Among angels are also those who are in charge of the trial of the grave. They are called Munkar and Nakir. Al-Bukhari (may Allah have mercy on him) transmitted from Anas (may Allah be pleased with him) that the Prophet (peace and blessings of Allah be upon him) said:

"When someone is placed in his grave, and his companions turn and go, and he can still hear the tread of their sandals, two angels come to him and make him sit up and say to him, `What do you say about this man, Mohammed (peace and blessings of Allah be upon him)? He will say, `I testify that he is the slave of Allah and His Messenger.' It will be said, `Look at your place in the Fire. Allah has given you, in exchange for it, a place in the Garden "The Prophet of Allah (peace and blessings of Allah be upon him) said,

"He will see both places."

"The unbeliever or the hypocrite will say, `I do not know. I used to say what everyone else said. He will be told, `You neither understood nor followed the guidance. Then he will be hit between the ears with an iron hammer and will cry out with a cry which is heard by everything near him except man and jinn."

Muslim reported something similar to it from Qatada (may Allah be pleased with him) and he added in it that Qatada said:

"He mentioned to us that the believer's grave will be expanded to about seventy cubits for him, and it will be filled with greenery until the day they are brought back to life."

Muslim transmitted from Abdullah bin `Abbas (may Allah be pleased with him) that the Messenger of Allah (peace and blessings of Allah be upon him) used to teach them their supplication in the same way that he used to teach them a *Surah* of Qur'an. He would say:

"O Allah, I seek refuge with You from the punishment of Hell and I seek refuge with You from the punishement of the grave. I seek refuge with You from the trial of the Masih (Christ) and Dajjal (Anti-Christ) and I seek refuge with You from the trials of life and death."

Garden and the Fire

Some of the angels are the custodians of the Garden. Their overseer is called **Ridwan** (peace be upon him).

Allah Almighty says :

وَسِيقَ الَّذِينَ اتَّقَوْا رَبَّهُمْ إِلَى الْجَنَّةِ زُمَرًا
حَتَّى إِذَا جَاءُوهَا وَفُتِحَتْ أَبْوَابُهَا وَقَالَ لَهُمْ خَزَنَتُهَا
سَلَامٌ عَلَيْكُمْ طِبْتُمْ فَادْخُلُوهَا خَالِدِينَ

"And those who feared their Lord will be led to the Garden in groups : until behold, they arrive there; its gate will be opened; and the Keepers will say: Peace be upon you! Well have ye done! Enter ye hear, to dweil therein." (Q. 39:73)

That is, the righteous ones will also go in crowds, and not be alone. There is now a true sorting out.

Then angels in heaven are not surprised at the advent of the good and righteous souls. They are glad; they greet them with the salutation of Peace; they congratulate them; and they welcome them within.

Ibn Kathir said:

"The custodian of the Garden is an angel called Ridwan. This is explicity stated in some *hadiths*."

There are also angels whose task is to give good news to the believers both at the time of their death and on the Day of Rising as the Almighty says :

اِنَّ الَّذِينَ قَالُوا رَبُّنَا اللهُ ثُمَّ اسْتَقَامُوا تَتَنَزَّلُ عَلَيْهِمُ الْمَلَئِكَةُ اَلَّا تَخَافُوا وَلَا تَحْزَنُوا وَاَبْشِرُوا بِالْجَنَّةِ الَّتِي كُنْتُمْ تُوعَدُونَ ۞ نَحْنُ اَوْلِيَٰؤُكُمْ فِى الْحَيوةِ الدُّنْيَا وَفِى الْاخِرَةِ وَلَكُمْ فِيهَا مَا تَشْتَهِى اَنْفُسُكُمْ وَلَكُمْ فِيهَا مَا تَدَّعُونَ ۞ نُزُلًا مِّنْ غَفُورٍ رَّحِيمٍ

"In the case of those who say, "Our Lord is Allah." And further, stand straight and steadfast, the angels descend on them (from time to time):

"Fear ye not!" (they suggest,) nor grieve! But receive the Glad Tidings of the Garden (of Bliss) the which ye were promised!

"We are your protectors in this life and in the Hereafter: therein shall ye have all that you shall desire; therein shall have all that ye ask for !

"A hospitable gift from one oft-forgetting, Most Merciful."   (Q. 41:30-32)

That is, the people who succeed in Eternal Life are those who recognise and understand the one and only Eternal Reality, that is Allah, and further shape their probationary Life firmly and steadfastly on the principles of the Truth and Reality. They will have their friends and protectors in the good angels, in contrast to the evil ones, who will have no friendship or protection, but only the reproaches of the Satan.

The Judgement and balancing of accounts will be a mighty Terror to the evildoers. But it will cause, to the righteous, not grief or anxiety, but hope and happiness, for now they will be in congenial atmosphere and will see the fulfilment of their ideals in the meeting and greeting of the angels, preparatory to their enjoyment of the supreme Bliss-seeing the Face of Allah.

Allah Almighty says :

لٰكِنِ الَّذِيْنَ اتَّقَوْا رَبَّهُمْ لَهُمْ جَنّٰتٌ تَجْرِيْ مِنْ تَحْتِهَا الْاَنْهٰرُ خٰلِدِيْنَ فِيْهَا نُزُلًا مِنْ عِنْدِ اللّٰهِ ۗ وَمَا عِنْدَ اللّٰهِ خَيْرٌ لِّلْاَبْرَارِ

"On the other hand, for those who feared their Lord, are guardens with rivers flowig beneath; therein are they to dwell (for ever), --an entertainment from Allah; and that which is from Allah is the best (Bliss) for the righteous." (Q. 1:198)

Ibn Abi Hatim said in this **isnad** from J'afar ibn Sulaiman who said that he heard Thabit recite **Sura Fussilat** until he reached, "those who say, "Our Lord is Allah", and then go straight, the angels descend on them." Then he stopped and said: "It has reached us that when Allah Almighty raises the believing slave from his grave, he will be met by the two angels who were with him in this world. They will say to him, `Feel no fear and do not be sad but rejoice in the Garden which you were promised." He said:

"Allah will give him security from his fear and delight his eye. None of the terrible things which people fear on the Day of Rising will be anything other than a delight for a believer due to the fact that Allah Almighty guided him, and on account of what he used to do for Him in this world."

They also include the custodians of Hell. We seek refuge with Allah from them! Its overseer is Malik.

Allah Almighty says about the people of the Fire:

وَنَادَوْا يٰمٰلِكُ لِيَقْضِ عَلَيْنَا رَبُّكَ ۖ قَالَ إِنَّكُمْ مَّاكِثُوْنَ

"They will cry out : "O Malik! Would that thy Lord put an end to us!" He will say, "Nay but ye shall abide!"   (Q. 43:77)

Malik is the name of the Angel incharge of the Hell. To the wrong-doers annihilation is better than agony. But wrong doers cannot destroy the "fruits" of their actions, by asking for annihilation.

Allah Almighty says:

إِنَّهُ مَنْ يَّأْتِ رَبَّهُ مُجْرِمًا فَإِنَّ لَهُ جَهَنَّمَ لَا يَمُوتُ فِيهَا وَلَا يَحْيَى

"Verily he who comes to his Lord as a sinner (at Judgement), -- for him is Hell : therein shall he neither die nor live."
(Q. 20:74)

Allah Almighty says:

وَقَالَ الَّذِينَ فِي النَّارِ لِخَزَنَةِ جَهَنَّمَ ادْعُوا رَبَّكُمْ يُخَفِّفْ
عَنَّا يَوْمًا مِّنَ الْعَذَابِ ۞   قَالُوا أَوَلَمْ تَكُ تَأْتِيكُمْ
رُسُلُكُمْ بِالْبَيِّنَاتِ قَالُوا بَلَى   قَالُوا فَادْعُوا وَمَا دُعَاؤُا
الْكَافِرِينَ إِلَّا فِي ضَلَالٍ ۞

"Those in the Fire will say : "Did there not come to you your Messengers with Clear Signs?" They will say, "Yes". They will reply, "Then pray (as ye like); But the prayer of those without Faith is nothing but (futile wandering) in mazes of error!"   (Q. 40:49-50)

The poor misguided ones will turn to the angels who are their Keepers, asking them to pray and intercede for them. But the angels are set there to watch over them, not to intercede for them. In their innocence they ask, `Did you have no warnings from Messengers, men like yourselves, in your past life?"

Here the answer being in the affirmative, they will have to tell the dreadful truth: This is neither the time nor the place for prayer, for mercy! And in any case, Prayer without Faith is Delusion, and must miss the mark.

Allah Almighty says:

لَهُ دَعْوَةُ الْحَقِّ وَالَّذِينَ يَدْعُونَ مِنْ دُونِهِ لَا يَسْتَجِيبُونَ لَهُمْ بِشَىْءٍ إِلَّا كَبَاسِطِ كَفَّيْهِ إِلَى الْمَاءِ لِيَبْلُغَ فَاهُ وَمَاهُوَ بِبَالِغِهِ وَمَادُعَاءُ الْكَافِرِينَ إِلَّا فِى ضَلَالٍ

"To Him is due the true prayer any others that they call upon besides Him hear them no more than if they were to stretch for their hands for water to reach their mouths but it reaches them not: for the prayer of those without Faith is nothing but vain prayer." (Q. 13:14)

Haqq = truth; right; what is due, befitting, proper. All these meanings are to be understood here. If we worship anything other than Allah (whether it is idols, stars, powers of nature, spirits or deified men, or self, or Power, or Wealth, Science or Art, Talent or Intellect), our worship is both foolish and futile.

Without Faith, it is obvious that prayer and worship has no meaning whatever. It is but an aberration of the mind. But there is a deeper meaning. You may have false faith, as in superstitions or in worshipping things other than Allah. In that case, too, you are persuing mere phantoms of the mind. When you come to examine it, it is more imbecility of futility. Worship and prayer are justified only to Allah, the One true God.

Allah Almighty says:

يَاأَيُّهَا الَّذِينَ آمَنُوا قُوا أَنْفُسَكُمْ وَأَهْلِيكُمْ نَارًا وَّقُودُهَا النَّاسُ وَالْحِجَارَةُ عَلَيْهَا مَلَائِكَةٌ غِلَاظٌ شِدَادٌ لَا يَعْصُونَ اللَّهَ مَا أَمَرَهُمْ وَيَفْعَلُونَ مَايُؤْمَرُونَ

"O ye who believe! Save yourselves and your families from a Fire whose fuel is Men and stones, over which are (appointed) Angels stern (and) severe, who flinch not (from executing) the commands they receive from Allah, but do (precisely) what they are commanded."   (Q. 66:6)

Note how we have been gradually led up in admonition from two consorts to all consorts, to all women, to all Believers, and to all men and women. We must carefully guard not only our own conduct, but the conduct of our families, and of all who are near and dear to us. For the issues are most serious, and the consequences of a fall are most terrible.

"A Fire whose Fuel is Men and Stones." This is terrible Fire: not merely like the physical fire which burns wood or charcoal or substances like that, and consumes them. This Fire will have for its fuel men who do wrong and are as hard hearted as stones, or Idols as symbolical of all the unbending Falsehood in life.

We think of the angel nature as gentle and beautiful, but in another aspect perfection includes justice, fidelity, discipline, and the firm execution of duty according to lawful Commands. So, in the attirbutes of Allah Himself, Justice and Mercy, Kindness and Correction are not contradictory but complementary. An earthly ruler will be unkind to his loyal subjects if he does not punish evil-doers.

Allah Almighty say :

فَإِن لَّمْ تَفْعَلُوا وَلَن تَفْعَلُوا فَٱتَّقُوا ٱلنَّارَ ٱلَّتِي وَقُودُهَا ٱلنَّاسُ وَٱلْحِجَارَةُ أُعِدَّتْ لِلْكَٰفِرِينَ ۝

"But if ye cannot -- and of a surety ye cannot -- then fear the Fire whose fuel is Men and stones which is prepared for those who reject Faith."   (Q. 2:24)

According to Commentators the "Stones" mentioned in this

verse refers to the idols which the polytheists worshipped. Thus, far from coming to the aid of their worshippers, the false gods would be a means of aggravating their torment.

Allah Almighty say :

وَمَآ أَدۡرَىٰكَ مَا سَقَرُ ۞ لَا تُبۡقِىٰ وَ لَا تَذَرُ ۞ لَوَّاحَةٌ لِّلۡبَشَرِ ۞
عَلَيۡهَا تِسۡعَةَ عَشَرَ ۞ وَمَا جَعَلۡنَآ أَصۡحَٰبَ النَّارِ الَّا مَلَٰٓئِكَةً وَّمَا جَعَلۡنَا
عِدَّتَهُمۡ إِلَّا فِتۡنَةً لِّلَّذِيۡنَ كَفَرُوۡا وَلِيَسۡتَيۡقِنَ الَّذِيۡنَ أُوتُوا الۡكِتَٰبَ وَيَزۡدَادَ
الَّذِيۡنَ اٰمَنُوۡٓا إِيۡمَانًا وَّلَا يَرۡتَابَ الَّذِيۡنَ أُوتُوا الۡكِتَٰبَ وَالۡمُؤۡمِنُوۡنَ وَلِيَقُوۡلَ
الَّذِيۡنَ فِىۡ قُلُوۡبِهِمۡ مَّرَضٌ وَّالۡكٰفِرُوۡنَ مَاذَآ أَرَادَ اللّٰهُ بِهٰذَا مَثَلًا كَذٰلِكَ
يُضِلُّ اللّٰهُ مَنۡ يَّشَآءُ وَيَهۡدِىۡ مَنۡ يَّشَآءُ وَمَا يَعۡلَمُ جُنُوۡدَ رَبِّكَ إِلَّا هُوَ
وَمَا هِىَ إِلَّا ذِكۡرَىٰ لِلۡبَشَرِ ۞

"And what will explain to thee what Hell-Fire is? Naught doth it permit to endure and naught doth it leave alone! -- darkening and changing the colour of man! Over it are Nineteen. And We have set none but angels as guardians of the Fire; and We have fixed their number only as a trial for Unbelievers, --- in order that the People of the Book may arrive at certainty, and the Believers may increase in Faith - and that no doubts may be left for the people of the Book and the believers, and that those in whose hearts is a disease and the Unbelievers may say, "What doth Allah intend by this?" Thus doth Allah leave to stray whom He pleaseth, and guide whom He pleaseth: and none can know the forces of thy Lord, except He, and this is no other than a warming to mankind." (Q. 74:27-31)

That is, he is in a state in which he neither lives nor dies. Looked at in another way, the things that in a good man are meant to last and grow, are for the sinner destroyed, and no part of his nature is left untouched. The brightness of his very manhood is darkened and extinguished by sin.

The figure nineteen refers to angels appointed to guard Hell.

There was a great volume of angelology in the religious literature of the People of the Book (i.e., the Jews and Christians) to whom (among others) an appeal is made in the verse. The Essence, a Jewish brotherhood with highly spiritual ideas, to which perhaps Prophet Jesus himself belonged, had an extensive literature of angelology. In the Midrash also which was Jewish school of exegesis and mystical interpretation there was much said about Angels. The Eastern Christians sects contemporary with the birth of Islam had borrowed and developed many of these ideas, and their mystics owed much to the Gnostics and the Persian apocalyptic systems. In the New Testament the relation of the Angels with Fire is referred to more than once.

We find in the *Sahih* of Muslim;

"On the Day of Rising, Hell will be drawn up by 70,000 thongs, and on each thong there will be 70,000 angels."

The Bearers of the Throne

Allah Almighty say :

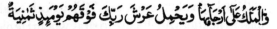

"And the angels will be on its sides, and eight will, that Day, bear the Throne of thy Lord above them."   (Q. 69:17)

The number eight has perhaps no special significance, unless it be with reference to the shape of the Throne or the number of the angels. The Oriental Throne is often octagonal, and its bearers would be one at each corner.

Ibn Abbas (may Allah be pleased with him) said that it means eight rows of angels.

From Jabir ibn Abdullah (may Allah be pleased with him) is that the Messenger of Allah (peace and blessings of Allah be upon him) said :

> "I was given permission to report about one of the angels of Allah Almighty among the Throne-bearers that between his ear-lobe and his neck is the distance of seven hundred years."

Dealings with the Sperm

Abdullah bin Mas'ud (may Allah be pleased with him) reports the Messenger of Allah (peace and blessings of Allah be upon him) to have said:

> "The way that each of you is created is that you are gathered in our mother's womb for forty days as a sperm-drop and then for a similar length of time as a lump of flesh. Then an Angel is sent and he breathes the spirit into you and is charged with four commands: to write down your provision, your life span, your actions, and whether you will be wretched or happy."

Anas bin Malik (may Allah be pleased with him) is reported to have said that the Messenger of Allah (peace and blessings of Allah be upon him) said:

> "Allah has put an angel incharge of the womb. He says: `O Lord, a drop? O Lord, a clot? O Lord, a morsel?' When Allah desires to complete the creation of the foetus, he says, O Lord, male or female? Wretched or happy? How much provision? How long a lifespan?' And he writes that for him

in mother's womb."

It is also related that these scribes write this between the eyes of the foetus. In the *isnad* of al-Bazzar from Ibn ʿUmar (may Allah be pleased with him) is that the Prophet (peace and blessings of Allah be upon him) said:

> "When Allah Almighty creates a living soul, the angel of the womb say, ʿO Lord, male or female?' "He said, "Allah decides it for him. Then he says, ʿO Lord, wretched or happy?' And Allah decides it for him. Then he writes between his eyes all he will encounter until his end overtakes him."

The Kurubiyyan

They include another category called *Kurubiyyan* They are the chiefs of the angels who are brought near and are the closest angels to the Throne-bearers.

The word *Kurubiyyan* comes from the root of *Kurb* which means sorrow, and they are called this on account of the intensity of their fear of Allah Almighty and their awe of Him: It is also said that the word is derived from the expression *Kurb* meaning nearness or strength in which case the name is due to their strength and stead-fastness in worship.

The Angel of the Mountains

One angel is entrusted with the mountains

Death of Abu Talib signalled the beginning of a difficult time for the Apostle. None of the Qurayshite dared touch the Prophet of Allah (peace and blessings of Allah be upon him) during the lifetime of Abu Talib but now the restraint was gone. Once, dust was thrown on his head. The Quraysh insulted and mocked at the Apostle and made caustic remarks on Islam. When the pagans persisted with their scoffs and scorns and contumacious behaviour, the Apostle thought of going to Ta'if to seek the help of Thaqif. The Prophet of Allah (peace and blessings of Allah be upon him) intended to invite them to Islam for he hoped that they would receive his message with sympathy. His expectation was apparently well-grounded as he has spent his childhood with Bani S'ad, who were settled near Ta'if. Ta'if was a delightful city, only next to Makkah in its population and prosperity, holding an important position in the Peninsula as alluded to in this verse of the Qur'an :

وَقَالُوالَوْلَا نُزِّلَ هَذَا الْقُرْانُ عَلَىٰ رَجُلٍ مِّنَ الْقَرْيَتَيْنِ عَظِيمٍ

"And they say : If only Qur'an had been revealed to some great men of two towns (Makkah and Ta'if)?" (Q. 43:31)

Ta'if was also a religious centre; the temple of *al-Lat* in that city was visited by pilgrims from every part of the country and, thus, it vied with Makkah which housed Hubal, the chief deity of Arabia. Ta'if was, as it still is, the summer resort of the Makkan aristrocrasy.

The inhabitants of Ta'if, endowed with large cultivations and vineyards, were wealthy and prosperous. They had become conceited and boastful answering the following discription of the anic verses :

وَمَآ أَرْسَلْنَا فِى قَرْيَةٍ مِّن نَّذِيرٍ إِلَّا قَالَ مُتْرَفُوهَآ
إِنَّا بِمَآ أُرْسِلْتُم بِهِ كَافِرُونَ

"And We sent not unto any township a warner, but the wealthy ones among them declared : Lo! We believe not in, that which ye bring unto us   (Q. 34:35)

وَقَالُوا نَحْنُ أَكْثَرُ أَمْوَالًا وَأَوْلَادًا وَمَا نَحْنُ بِمُعَذَّبِينَ

"And they say: We are more (than you) in wealth and
children. We are not to be punished!"   (Q.34:35)

In Ta'if the Apostle first met the chiefs and leaders of Thaqif
whom he invited to accept Islam. They were, however, rude and
discourteous in their behaviour to the Apostle. Not being content
with their insolent reply, they even stirred up some rebble of the
town to harass the Apostle. These riff-raffs followed the Apostle,
abusing and crying and throwing stones on him, until he was
compelled to take refuge in an orchard. The Apostle had thus to
endure even more troubles in Ta'if than he had to face in Makkah.
These louts standing on either side of the path threw stones on him
until his feet were injured and smeared with blood. Their oppres-
sion so weighed upon the |Apostle that in a state of depression a
prayer complaining about his helplessness and pitiable condition
and seeking the succour of Allah came to his lips.

"O Allah", said the Prophet, to Thee I complain of my
weakness, resourcelessness and humiliation before the
people. Thou art the most Merciful, the Lord of weak and
my Master. To whom wilt Thou confide me? To one
estranged, bearing ill will, or an enemy given power over
me? If Thou art not in wrath on me, I care not, for Thy favour
is abundant for me. I seek refuge in the light of Thy
countenance by which all darkness is dispelled and every
affair of this world and the next is set right, lest Thy anger
should descend upon me or Thy displeasure light upon me.
I need only Thy pleasure and satisfaction for only Thou
enablest me to do good and erase the evil. There is no
power and no might save in Thee.

"The Lord then sent the angel of mountains who soght
the Prophet's permission to join together the two hills

between which Ta'if was located but the Messenger of Allah replied, " No, I hope Allah will bring forth from their loins people who worship Allah alone, associating nothing with Him."

*(Muslim, **Kitab-ul-Jihad**).*

The Angels of the Ranks

They include the Angels of the ranks who do not slacken in worship, those who stand and do not bow, those who bow, and those who prostrate and do not come up from their prostration. And there are others who are different from any of these :

وَمَا يَعْلَمُ جُنُودَ رَبِّكَ إِلَّا هُوَ وَمَا هِىَ إِلَّا ذِكْرَى لِلْبَشَرِ

"And none can know the forces of thy Lord, except He, and this is no other than a warming to mankind." (Q. 74:31).

It is necessary consequences of moral responsibility and freedom of choice in man, that he should be left free to stray if he chooses to do so, inspite of all the warning and the instruction he receives. Allah's channels of warning and instruction--his spiritual forces--are infinite as are His powers. No man can know them. But this warning or reminder is addressed to all mankind.

Allah Almighty says :

مَا أَصَابَكَ مِنْ حَسَنَةٍ فَمِنَ اللهِ وَمَا أَصَابَكَ مِنْ سَيِّئَةٍ فَمِنْ نَفْسِكَ وَأَرْسَلْنَاكَ لِلنَّاسِ رَسُولًا وَكَفَى بِاللهِ شَهِيدًا

Whatever good, (O man!) happens to thee, is from Allah; but whatever evil happens to thee, is from thyself and We have sent thee as a Messenger to (instruct) mankind. And enough is Allah for a witness."   (Q. 4:79).

To blame a man of God for our misfortunes is doubly unjust.

For he comes to save us from misfortune, and it is because we flout him or pay no heed to him, that our own rebellion brings its own punishment. If we realise this truth we shall be saved from two sins:

(1) the sin of injustice to Allah's Messengers, who came for our good, and not for our harm:

(2) the sin of not realising our own shortcomings or rebellion, and thus living in spiritual darkness. If the Message is from Allah, that carries its own authority: "Enough is Allah for a witness."

Musnad and *Tirmidhi* from Abu Dhar (may Allah be pleased with him) that the Messenger of Allah (peace and blessings of Allah be upon him) said:

"I see what you do not see and I hear that you do not hear. The heaven groans and it has a right to groan. There is no place in it the size of four fingers which does not have an angel prostrating in it. If you knew what I know, you would laugh little and weep much and not enjoy women in your beds and you would go out to the hill crying out to Allah Almighty and Exalted.

The meaning of "the heaven groans" is that it makes the sound of the creaking of a saddle which is placed on the camel's back, i.e., due to the great number of the angels in it, which weighs it down so that it groans.

The Angels of Dhikr

Yet another type is the travelling angels who seek gatherings of **dhikr**. Abu Hurairah (may Allah be pleased with him) reports that the Messenger of Allah (peace and blessings of Allah be upon him) said:

"Allah Almighty has angels who roam about seeking the people of **dhikr** of Allah, they call to one another, `come to that which you have been seeking!' And they beat their wings and fly up to the nearest heaven. Then their Lord questions them---and He knows better:--
`What do My slaves say?'
They glorify and proclaim You great, praise You and magnify You. They say.
Have they seen Me?' He says then.
`No, by Allah, they have not seen You.' they say
`And how would it be if they did see Me?' He says then.

`If they did see You, they would be even stronger in worshipping You, stronger in glorifying You, and stronger in magnifying You."
`And what do They ask of Me?' He says
`They ask you for the Garden'. they say.
`And have they seen it?' He says.

`No, by Allah, they have not seen it', they say. "Then how would it be if they had seen it?' He says.

`If they had seen it they would be all the stronger in their striving for it, stronger in their seeking it, and stronger in their desire for it.' they say, `Then from what do they seek deliverence?' He says.
`From the Fire', they say.
`Then how would it be if they saw it?' He says.

`If they saw it, they would be the stronger in their flight from it and stronger in their fear for it', they say.
`I call you to witness that I have forgiven them.'
Among them is so-and-so, and he is not one of them.

He has only come for somethig which he needs', one of the

Angels says.

'They are companions of whom it can be said that no one who is their companion will be wretched'."

(Bukhari and *Muslim)*

Ibn Hajr said in the **Fath al-Bari**:

"This **hadith** shows the excellence of gatherings of **dhikr** and those who do **dhikr**, and the excellence of people gathering together for that reason, as well as the fact that anyone who sits with them is included along with them in all that Allah Almighty bestows on them to honour them, even if he does not participate with them in the *dhikr* itself. It also shows the love and concern of the angels for the tribe of Adam. It also contains the fact that the Questioner comes to the one who asks even though He has better knowledge of the one He asks about than the one who is asked. This is in order to show His concern for those He asks about, to praise their ability of their station.

"It is said that another of the features of Allah's asking the angels about the people of **dhikr** is to call attention to what they said when they said :

أَتَجْعَلُ فِيهَا مَنْ يُفْسِدُ فِيهَا وَيَسْفِكُ الدِّمَاءَ وَنَحْنُ نُسَبِّحُ بِحَمْدِكَ وَنُقَدِّسُ لَكَ

"Why place on it one who will corrupt it and shed blood when we glorify Your praise and call you holy?' (Q. 2:30)

`So it is as if He were saying to them. `Look at the glorification and proclamation of your holiness that comes from them inspite of the appetites and the whishpering of Satan which overpower them. See how they deal with that yet resemble you in respect of glorification and holy praise.

"It is said that also taken from this *hadith* is that the

dhikr of the tribe of Adam is more sublime and nobler than that of the angels since those descended from Adam manage to do *dhikr* in spite of the many preoccupations they have and the transactions they are involved in, while none of that is the case where the angels are concerned."

Angels Connected with Visions

Bukhari reports from Ayesha (may Allah be pleased with her) that the Messenger of Allah (peace and blessings of Allah be upon him) said:

> "I saw you twice in a dream before I married you. I saw an angel carrying you wrapped in a piece of silk and I said 'Unwrap it!' and it was unwrapped and there you were. I said, 'If this is from Allah, it will come about.'"

Ibn Hajr said:

> "Al-Qurtubi transmitted in *al-Mufham* from one of the people of Knowledge that Allah Almighty has an angel who presents the things seen in the sleeper's domain of perception and gives them sensory form so that sometimes there are likenes which correspond to already existing forms, and sometimes they are examples of intelligible meanings. In both cases there is either good news or warning."

Al-Hakim al-Tirmidhi said:

> "Allah has entrusted an angel with the business of visions. He learns the states of tribe of Adam from the Preserved Tablet, and then he copies it and coins a likeness of each according to particular archtype. When a person sleeps, he gives form the those things for him with wisdom so that it will be good news or warning or rebuke for him.

"The Adamic creature is overpowered by Satan to the intense enmity which exists between him and Satan, and so he tricks him in every possible way, and wants to corrupt his affairs in every possible way. therefore he muddles up his dreams, either by putting error into them or by making him forget them."

Ibn Hajr said:

"All dreams fall into two categories. The first are true dreams, which are the dreams of the Prophets and those of the righteous who follow them. They occur to others in rare cases. This is the type of dream when what happens in it corresponds to what happens in the waking state. The second consists of muddled dream which do not warn about anything. There are different types of these.

"One is the playing-about of Satan so that the dream is troubling. For instance someone might see his head cut off and himself chasing it or dream that he falls into a state of terror and has no one to rescue him from it and other such-like things. Another is when someone sees one of the angels commanding him to do something *haram*, for instance. Dreams like this present logical impossiblities.

"A third is when someone sees the same sort of things his self says to him when he is awake or that he desires something, sees it when he is asleep, like when he dreams of something which normally occurs in the wakening state or of something that dominates his nature. This kind of dream occurs mostly about the future, sometimes about the present and only rarely about the past."

Various Forms of Angels

The angels are free to take any shape of like other than their true form. They appear to a selected elite of the slaves of Allah, frequently in the shape of extraordinary men with handsome forms and shining faces and excellent clothes. However the bodies they take on when adopting human form do not remove them from the basic nature they were given by Allah when He created them. Thus when, for instance, they take on human form, human nature does not have any power over them. They do not, for example, eat or drink.

The angels appear to the close Friend of the Merciful, Hazrat Ibrahim (peace be upon him), in this Adamic form which led him, due to the impulse of generosity rooted in his basic nature, to hasten to offer them hospitability, thinking that they were ordinary guests. They came to him to visit him.

Allah Almighty says ·

هَلْ اَتٰىكَ حَدِيثُ ضَيْفِ اِبْرٰهِيْمَ الْمُكْرَمِيْنَ ۞ اِذْ دَخَلُوْا عَلَيْهِ
فَقَالُوْا سَلٰمًا قَالَ سَلٰمٌ قَوْمٌ مُّنْكَرُوْنَ ۞ فَرَاغَ اِلٰٓى اَهْلِهٖ فَجَآءَ بِعِجْلٍ
سَمِيْنٍ ۞ فَقَرَّبَهٗ اِلَيْهِمْ قَالَ اَلَا تَأْكُلُوْنَ ۞ فَاَوْجَسَ مِنْهُمْ خِيْفَةً ؕ
قَالُوْا لَا تَخَفْ ؕ وَبَشَّرُوْهُ بِغُلٰمٍ عَلِيْمٍ ۞ فَاَقْبَلَتِ امْرَاَتُهٗ فِىْ صَرَّةٍ فَصَكَّتْ
وَجْهَهَا وَقَالَتْ عَجُوْزٌ عَقِيْمٌ ۞ قَالُوْا كَذٰلِكِ ۙ قَالَ رَبُّكِ ؕ اِنَّهٗ هُوَ
الْحَكِيْمُ الْعَلِيْمُ ۞ قَالَ فَمَا خَطْبُكُمْ اَيُّهَا الْمُرْسَلُوْنَ ۞
قَالُوْٓا اِنَّآ اُرْسِلْنَآ اِلٰى قَوْمٍ مُّجْرِمِيْنَ ۞ لِنُرْسِلَ عَلَيْهِمْ حِجَارَةً مِّنْ طِيْنٍ ۞
مُّسَوَّمَةً عِنْدَ رَبِّكَ لِلْمُسْرِفِيْنَ

'Has the story reached thee, of the honoured guests of

Abraham? Behold, they entered his presence and said:
"Peace!" He said, "Peace" (And thought, "These seem)
unknown people." Then he turned quickly to his household,
brought out a fatted calf, and placed it before them ..... he
said, "will ye not eat?" (When they did not eat), he conceived
a fear of them. They said, "Fear not," and they gave him glad
tidings of a son endowed with knowledge. But his wife came
forward clamouring: she smote her forehead and said: "A
barren old woman!" They said, "Even so has thy Lord
spoken: And He is full of Wisdom and knowledge."
(Abraham) said : "And what, O ye Messenger, is your
errand (now)? They said, "We have been sent to a people
(deep) in sin; -- to bring on, on them, (a shower of) stones
of clay (brimstone), marked as from the Lord for those who
trespass beyond bounds." (Q. 51:24-34).

Allah Almighty says :

وَلَقَدْ جَاءَتْ رُسُلُنَا إِبْرَٰهِيمَ بِالْبُشْرَىٰ قَالُوا سَلَٰمًا
قَالَ سَلَٰمٌ فَمَا لَبِثَ أَن جَآءَ بِعِجْلٍ حَنِيذٍ ۞ فَلَمَّا رَآ أَيْدِيَهُمْ
لَا تَصِلُ إِلَيْهِ نَكِرَهُمْ وَأَوْجَسَ مِنْهُمْ خِيفَةً قَالُوا لَا تَخَفْ إِنَّا
أُرْسِلْنَا إِلَىٰ قَوْمِ لُوطٍ ۞ وَامْرَأَتُهُ قَآئِمَةٌ فَضَحِكَتْ فَبَشَّرْنَٰهَا
بِإِسْحَٰقَ وَمِن وَرَآءِ إِسْحَٰقَ يَعْقُوبَ ۞ قَالَتْ يَٰوَيْلَتَىٰٓ ءَأَلِدُ
وَأَنَا۠ عَجُوزٌ وَهَٰذَا بَعْلِى شَيْخًا إِنَّ هَٰذَا لَشَىْءٌ عَجِيبٌ ۞
قَالُوٓا أَتَعْجَبِينَ مِنْ أَمْرِ اللَّهِ رَحْمَتُ اللَّهِ وَبَرَكَٰتُهُ عَلَيْكُمْ أَهْلَ
الْبَيْتِ إِنَّهُ حَمِيدٌ مَّجِيدٌ

"There came our Messengers to Abraham with glad tidings.
They said, "Peace!" He answered, "Peace!" and hastened to
entertain them with a roasted calf. But when he saw their
hands not reaching towards the (meal), he felt some mistrust
of them, and conceived a fear of them. They said: "Fear not

we have been sent against the people of Lut. And his wife
was standing (there), and she laughed: but We gave her glad
tidings of Isasc, and after him, of Jacob. She said: "Alas for
me! shall I bear a child, seeing I am an old woman and my
husband here is an old man? That would indeed be a
wonderful thing!" They said: "Dost thou wonder at Allah's
decree? The grace of Allah and His blessings on you, O ye
peple of the house! For He is indeed worthy of all praise,
full of all glory!"   (Q. 11:69-73)

It is introduced by a chief reference to an episode in the life
of his uncle Abraham, from whose seed sprang the peoples to
whom Moses, Jesus and Mohammed Al-Mustafa were sent with
the major Revelations. Abraham had by this time passed through
the fire of persecutions in the Mesopotamian valleys: he had left
behind him the ancestral idolatory of Ur of the Chaldees; he had
been tried and he had truimphed over the persecution of Nimrud:
he had not taken up his residence in Canaan, from which his
nephew Lot (Lut) was called to preach to the wicked cities of the
Plain east of the Dead sea which is itself called Bahr Lut. Thus
prepared and sanctified, he was now ready to receive the Message that he was chosen to be the progenitor of a great line of
Prophets, and that Message is now referred to.

Can we localise Nimrud? If local tradition in place-names
can be relied upon, this king must have ruled over the tract
which includes the modern Nimrud, on the Tigris, about
twenty miles south of Mosul. This is the site of Assyrian ruins
of great interest, but the rise of Assyrian as an Empire was
of course much later time than the time of Abraham. The
Assyrian city was called Kalakh (Calah), and archaelogical
excavations carried out there have yielded valuable results,
which are, however, irrelevant for our commentary.

Abraham received the strangers with a salutation of Peace, and immediately placed before them sumptuous meal of roasted calf and strangers were embarrassed. They were angels and did not eat. If hospitality is refused, it means that those who refuse it must have no good to the would be host. Abraham therefore had a feeling of mistrust and fear in his mind, which the strangers at once set at rest by saying that their mission was in the first place to help Lut as a warner to the Cities of Plain. But in the second place they had good news for Abraham: he was to be the father of great peoples'.

The narrative is very concise, and most of the details are taken for granted. We may suppose that the angels gave the news first to Abraham who is already a hundred years of age, and his wife Sarah was not far short of ninety. She was probably screened. She could hardly believed in the news. In her scepticism (some say in her joy) she laughed. But the news was formally communicated to her that she was to be mother of Issac, and through Issac, the grand mother of Jacob. Jacob was to be a fruitful, with his twelve sons. But hitherto Abraham had no son by her, and Sarah was passed the age of child-bearing. "How could it be?" He thought.

This little episode of Abraham's life comes in fitly as one of the illustrations of Allah's wonderful providence in His dealings with man. Abraham had tussle with his father on behalf of Truth and Unity, he had passed through the fire unscathed; he had travelled to far countries, and was now ready to receive his great mission as the fountainhead of Prophets in his old age. Humanly speaking, it seemed impossible that he should have a son at his age, and yet it came to pass and became a corner-stone of sacred history.

In illustration of the contrasts between Good and Evil, and the consequences that flow from them, we have now a reference to four incidents from the past, viz., : (1) an incident from the story of

Abraham; (2) from that of Lot, nephew of Abraham, and the end of the Cities of the Plain, which he was sent to warn; (3) the people of the Wood; and (4) the people of the Rocky Tract (Hijr), after whom this is called. As usual, the recital of Allah's abounding grace comes first.

For a full understanding of this reference to the angels who were Abraham's guests and came to announce the birth of a son to him in the old age. The appearance of two strangers of uncommon appearance, who refused to partake of the host's sumptuous hospitality, made Abraham at first suspicious and afraid.

The birth of a son in old age, to a sonless father was glad tidings for Abraham personally. The birth of a son endowed with wisdom promised something infinitely more. Considering that the angels were divine wisdom, and the event became an event of prime importance in the world's religious history. For Abraham, became through his progeny the root of the three great universal religions diffused throughtout the world.

The holy Qur'an says :

فَلَمَّا جَآءَ اٰلَ لُوطٍ الْمُرْسَلُونَ ۞ قَالَ اِنَّكُمْ قَوْمٌ مُّنكَرُونَ ۞ قَالُوا بَلْ جِئْنَاكَ بِمَا كَانُوا فِيهِ يَمْتَرُونَ

"At length when the Messengers arrived among the adherents of Lut. He said, "Ye appeared to be uncommon folk."   (Q. 15:61-62)

The unusual appearance of the angels struck Lut as it had struck Abraham. Knowing the abominable vices to which the Cities were addicted, he feared to entertain handsome young men. They at once disclosed their mission to him. In effect they said: "You, Lut, have been preaching in vain to these wicked Cities.

When you warn them of their inevitable end. Destruction, they laugh and doubt. Now their doubt will be resolved. Their destruction will be accompanied before the morning."

They were addicted to unnatural crime, and the news of the advent of handsome young men inflamed them. How true it is that at the very verge of destruction, men rush blindly to their fate, and cut off any last hope of repentance and mercy for themselves.

Lut, the only righteous man in the City, had frequently remonstrated with the inhabitants against their unnatural crimes, and they had forbidden him to speak to them agian on behalf of any one, "as if" (they might tauntingly say) he was the protector of all and sundry."

Allah Almighty says :

وَلَمَّا جَآءَتْ رُسُلُنَا لُوطاً سِىٓءَ بِهِمْ وَضَاقَ بِهِمْ ذَرْعاً وَقَالَ هٰذَا يَوْمٌ عَصِيبٌ ۞ وَجَآءَهُ قَوْمُهُ يُهْرَعُونَ إِلَيْهِ وَمِنْ قَبْلُ كَانُوا يَعْمَلُونَ السَّيِّاٰتِ قَالَ يٰقَوْمِ هٰٓؤُلَآءِ بَنَاتِىْ هُنَّ أَطْهَرُ لَكُمْ فَاتَّقُوا اللّٰهَ وَلَا تُخْزُونِ فِىْ ضَيْفِىْ أَلَيْسَ مِنْكُمْ رَجُلٌ رَّشِيْدٌ ۞ قَالُوْا لَقَدْ عَلِمْتَ مَالَنَا فِىْ بَنٰتِكَ مِنْ حَقٍّ وَإِنَّكَ لَتَعْلَمُ مَانُرِيْدُ ۞ قَالَ لَوْ أَنَّ لِىْ بِكُمْ قُوَّةً أَوْ اٰوِىْٓ إِلٰى رُكْنٍ شَدِيْدٍ ۞ قَالُوْا يٰلُوْطُ إِنَّا رُسُلُ رَبِّكَ لَنْ يَّصِلُوْٓا إِلَيْكَ فَأَسْرِ بِأَهْلِكَ بِقِطْعٍ مِّنَ الَّيْلِ وَلَا يَلْتَفِتْ مِنْكُمْ أَحَدٌ إِلَّا امْرَأَتَكَ إِنَّهُ مُصِيْبُهَا مَآ أَصَابَهُمْ إِنَّ مَوْعِدَهُمُ الصُّبْحُ أَلَيْسَ الصُّبْحُ بِقَرِيْبٍ ۞ فَلَمَّا جَآءَ أَمْرُنَا جَعَلْنَا عَالِيَهَا سَافِلَهَا وَأَمْطَرْنَا عَلَيْهَا حِجَارَةً مِّنْ سِجِّيْلٍ مَّنْضُوْدٍ ۞ مُّسَوَّمَةً عِنْدَ رَبِّكَ وَ مَاهِىَ مِنَ الظّٰلِمِيْنَ بِبَعِيْدٍ

"When our Messenger came to Lut, he was grieved on their

account and felt himself powerless (to protect them). He said: "This is a distressful day." And his people came rushing towards him, and they had been long in the habit of practising abominations. He said: "O my people! here are my daughters: they are purer for you (if ye marry)! Now fear Allah and cover me not with disgrace about my guests.' Is there not among you a single right-minded man?" They said: "Well dost thou know we have no need of thy daughters: indeed thou knowest quite well what we want!" He said: "Would that I had power to suppress you or that I could betake myself to some powerful support." (The messengers) said: "O Lut! we are Messengers from thy Lord! By no means shall they reach thee! Now travel with thy family while yet a part of the night remains, and let not any of you look back: but thy wife (will remain behind): to her will happen what happens to the people. Morning is their time appointed: Is not the mornig nigh?" When our decree issued, we turned (the cities) upside down and rained down on them brimstones hard as baked clay, spread, layer on layer, -- marked as from thy Lord: nor are they ever far from those who do wrong!" (Q. 11:77-83)

The story of Lut, as referred to in *surah* 7 *ayahs* 80-84 laid emphasis on the rejection of Lut's mission by men who practised unnatural abominations. Here the emphasis is laid on Allah's dealings with men -- in mercy for true spiritual service and the righteous and wrath and punishment for those who defy the laws of nature established by Him, --- also on men's dealings with each other and the contrast between the righteous and the wicked who respect no laws, human or divine.

The Biblical narrative suggests that the daughters were married and their husbands were close by and that these same daughters afterwards committed incest with their father and had children by him. The holy Qur'an nowhere suggests such abominations. Some Commentators suggest that "my daughters" in the mouth of a venarable man like Lut, the father of his people, may mean any young girls of those towns. "My son" (**waladi**) is still a common mode of address in Arabic-speaking countries when an elderly man addresses a young man.

Lut seemed helpless in the situation in which he found himself, -- alone against a rabble of people inflamed with evil passion. He wished he had the strength to suppress them himself or had some powerful support to lean on! But the powerful support was there, though he had not realised it till then. It was the support of Allah. His guests were not ordinary men, Angels who had come to test the people before they inflicted the punishment. They now declared themselves, and gave him directions to get away before the morning, when the punishment would descend on the doomed City of the plain.

Even in Lut's household was one who detracted from the harmony of the family. She was disobedient to her husband, and he was her husband obeying Allah's Command. She looked back and shared the fate of the wicked inhabitants of the Cities of the Plain:

The Holy Qur'an says :

وَأَمْطَرْنَا عَلَيْهِم مَّطَرًا فَانْظُرْ كَيْفَ كَانَ عَاقِبَةُ الْمُجْرِمِينَ ۞

"And we rained down on them a shower (of brimstone): then see what was the end of those who indulged in sin and crime!"   (Q. 7:84)

The shower is expressly stated in Q. XI. 82 to have been of stones. In XV: 73-74, we are told that was a terrible blast of noise (**saihat**) in addition to the shower of stones.

They : Arabic, *hiya*: some commentators take the pronoun to refer to the Wicked Cities so destroyed: the meaning then would be: these wicked cities were not so different from other cities that do wrong, for they would all suffer similar punishment! Perhaps it would be better to refer "they" to the stones of punishment by a metonymy for "punishment": punishment would not be far from any people that did wrong.

Maryam and the Angels

Allah Almighty says :

إِذْ قَالَتِ الْمَلَٰئِكَةُ يَٰمَرْيَمُ إِنَّ اللَّهَ يُبَشِّرُكِ بِكَلِمَةٍ مِّنْهُ ٱسْمُهُ الْمَسِيحُ عِيسَى ابْنُ مَرْيَمَ   وَجِيهًا فِى الدُّنْيَا وَالْآخِرَةِ وَمِنَ الْمُقَرَّبِينَ ۞ وَيُكَلِّمُ النَّاسَ فِى الْمَهْدِ وَكَهْلًا وَّمِنَ الصَّٰلِحِينَ ۞

"Recall when the angels said: O Mary, verily Allah gives thee glad tidings of a Word from Him; his name shall be Masih (Messiah), Isa (Jesus) son of Maryam (Mery) illustrious in the world and the Hereafter, and one of those granted nearness to Allah. And he shall speak to the people in the cradle and when of middle age; and shall be of the righteous."   (Q. 3:45-46)

Kalimah means a word, a decree, a command (Mufradat). The birth of Jesus was announced in one word "Be!" Mary would have conception without the help of any male person. In these words there is a clear repudiation of the Divinity of Jesus Christ. How can he be looked upon as god, and presumed to be a shareholder of Lord's Divinity when he has been created by the command of Allah.

Messiah of the Bible, the surname of Jesus, is a title of honour:

literally meaning the `anointed'. The designation **al-Masih** is the Arabianised form of the term frequently applied in the Bible to the Hebrew Kings, whose accession to power used to be consecrated by a touch with holy oil taken from the Temple.

It may also mean one who has a healing touch in him as Jesus cured the persons by his healing touch.

In these few words the holy Qur'an in its naturally superb style winnows out the mistaken notions of both the Christians and the Jews, and clarifies the status of Jesus Christ. Repudiatiating the Christians' claim of his being son of God, the Qur'an tells that it is inconsistent with the nature of his birth. He is born of the womb of a lady, how can then he be rightly clamied as the co-sharer in the Divinity of the Lord. The epithet of his being the son of Mary emphasized the fact of his humanness. The Qur'an vehemently repudiates the calummies of the Jews also and states that Jesus Christ is the illustrious son of an illustirous mother, very honourable and like all Prophets occupies an exalted place in the eye of Allah.

The mirculous aspect of Christ's talk was that he spoke to people in the cradle with extraordinary wisdom and knowledge as he spoke at the age of maturity. The mention of the two stages of his growth is meaningful as it stresses the obvious fact that he passed through these two stages of growth as all other mortals do pass.

Allah Almighty says :

وَاذْكُرْ فِى الْكِتَابِ مَرْيَمَ اِذِ انْتَبَذَتْ مِنْ اَهْلِهَا مَكَانًا شَرْقِيًّا ۞
فَاتَّخَذَتْ مِنْ دُوْنِهِمْ حِجَابًا ۚ فَاَرْسَلْنَآ اِلَيْهَا رُوْحَنَا فَتَمَثَّلَ
لَهَا بَشَرًا سَوِيًّا

"Relate in the Book (the story of) Mary, when she withdrew from her family to a place in the East. She placed a screen (to screen herself) from them: then We sent to her our angel, and he appeared before her as a man in all respects." (Q. 19:16-17)

The story of Mary as related in *Surah* iii *ayahs* 42-51. Here the whole theme is different: it is the personal side of the experience of the worshippers of Allah in relation to their families or environment.

To a private eastern chamber, perhaps in the Temple. She went into privacy from her people and from people in general, for prayer and devotion. It was in this state of purity that the angel appeared to her in the form of a man. She thought it was a man. She was frightened, and she adjured him not to invade her privacy.

Allah Almighty says :

وَإِذْ قَالَتِ الْمَلَٰٓئِكَةُ يَٰمَرْيَمُ إِنَّ اللَّهَ اصْطَفَىٰكِ وَطَهَّرَكِ وَاصْطَفَىٰكِ عَلَىٰ نِسَآءِ الْعَٰلَمِينَ ۞ يَٰمَرْيَمُ اقْنُتِي لِرَبِّكِ وَاسْجُدِي وَارْكَعِي مَعَ الرَّٰكِعِينَ ۞ ذَٰلِكَ مِنْ أَنۢبَآءِ الْغَيْبِ نُوحِيهِ إِلَيْكَ ۚ وَمَا كُنتَ لَدَيْهِمْ إِذْ يُلْقُونَ أَقْلَٰمَهُمْ أَيُّهُمْ يَكْفُلُ مَرْيَمَ وَمَا كُنتَ لَدَيْهِمْ إِذْ يَخْتَصِمُونَ

"Behold! the angels said: 'O Mary! Allah hath chosed thee and purified thee -- chosen thee above the women of all the nations. O Mary! worship the Lord devoutly, prostrate thyself, and bow down (in prayer) with those who bow down. 'This is the part of the tidings of the things unseen, which We reveal unto thee. (O Prophet!) by inspiration. Thou wast not with them when they cast lots with pens, as to which of them should be charged with the care of Mary;

nor was thou with them when they disputed (the point).

اِذْقَالَتِ الْمَلَٰٓئِكَةُ يَٰمَرْيَمُ اِنَّ اللّٰهَ يُبَشِّرُكِ بِكَلِمَةٍ مِّنْهُ ۖ
اسْمُهُ الْمَسِيحُ عِيْسَى ابْنُ مَرْيَمَ وَجِيهًا فِى الدُّنْيَا
وَالْاٰخِرَةِ وَمِنَ الْمُقَرَّبِينَ ۙ

"Behold! the angels said: O Mary! Allah giveth thee glad tidings of a Word from Him: his name will be Jesus Christ, the son of Mary held in honour of this world and the Hereafter and of (the company of) those nearest of Allah.

وَيُكَلِّمُ النَّاسَ فِى الْمَهْدِ وَكَهْلًا وَّمِنَ الطَّٰلِحِيْنَ ۞ قَالَتْ
رَبِّ اَنّٰى يَكُوْنُ لِى وَلَدٌ وَّلَمْ يَمْسَسْنِى بَشَرٌ ۖ قَالَ كَذٰلِكِ اللّٰهُ
يَخْلُقُ مَا يَشَآءُ ۚ اِذَا قَضٰٓى اَمْرًا فَاِنَّمَا يَقُوْلُ لَهُ كُنْ فَيَكُوْنُ

"He shall speak to the people in childhood and in maturity. And he shall be (of the company) of the righteous."

She said: "O my Lord! how shall I have a son when no man hath touched me?" He said: "Even so; Allah createht what He willeth: when He hath decreed a matter He but saith to it. `Be', and it is!

وَيُعَلِّمُهُ الْكِتٰبَ وَالْحِكْمَةَ وَالتَّوْرٰىةَ وَالْاِنْجِيْلَ ۚ وَرَسُوْلًا اِلٰى
بَنِىْ اِسْرَآءِيْلَ ۙ اَنِّىْ قَدْ جِئْتُكُمْ بِاٰيَةٍ مِّنْ رَّبِّكُمْ ۙ اَنِّىْ اَخْلُقُ
لَكُمْ مِّنَ الطِّيْنِ كَهَيْئَةِ الطَّيْرِ فَاَنْفُخُ فِيْهِ فَيَكُوْنُ طَيْرًا بِاِذْنِ
اللّٰهِ ۚ وَاُبْرِئُ الْاَكْمَهَ وَالْاَبْرَصَ وَاُحْيِ الْمَوْتٰى بِاِذْنِ اللّٰهِ ۚ وَ
اُنَبِّئُكُمْ بِمَا تَأْكُلُوْنَ وَمَا تَدَّخِرُوْنَ ۙ فِىْ بُيُوْتِكُمْ ۚ اِنَّ فِىْ ذٰلِكَ
لَاٰيَةً لَّكُمْ اِنْ كُنْتُمْ مُّؤْمِنِيْنَ

"And Allah will teach him the Book and the Wisdom, the Torah and the Gospel, and (appoint him) a Messenger to the Children of Israel, (with this message): "I have come to you, with Sign from your Lord, in that I make for you out of clay, as it were, the figure of a bird, and breathe into it, and it becomes a bird by Allah's leave: and I heal those born blind, and the lepers, and I bring dead to life by Allah's leave: and I declare to you what ye eat, and what ye store in your houses. Surely therein is a Sign for you if ye did believe.

وَمُصَدِّقًا لِّمَا بَيْنَ يَدَيَّ مِنَ التَّوْرَاةِ وَلِأُحِلَّ لَكُم بَعْضَ الَّذِي حُرِّمَ عَلَيْكُمْ وَجِئْتُكُم بِآيَةٍ مِّن رَّبِّكُمْ فَاتَّقُوا اللَّهَ وَأَطِيعُونِ ۝ إِنَّ اللَّهَ رَبِّي وَرَبُّكُمْ فَاعْبُدُوهُ هَٰذَا صِرَاطٌ مُّسْتَقِيمٌ ۝ فَلَمَّا أَحَسَّ عِيسَىٰ مِنْهُمُ الْكُفْرَ قَالَ مَنْ أَنصَارِي إِلَى اللَّهِ قَالَ الْحَوَارِيُّونَ نَحْنُ أَنصَارُ اللَّهِ آمَنَّا بِاللَّهِ وَاشْهَدْ بِأَنَّا مُسْلِمُونَ ۝ رَبَّنَا آمَنَّا بِمَا أَنزَلْتَ وَاتَّبَعْنَا الرَّسُولَ فَاكْتُبْنَا مَعَ الشَّاهِدِينَ ۝

"(I have come to you), to attest the Torah which was before me. And to make lawful to you part of what was (before) forbidden to you; I have come to you with a Sign from your Lord. So fear Allah, and obey me."

"It is Allah Who is my Lord and your Lord; then worship Him. This is a way that is straight."

"When Jesus found Unbelief on their part he said: "Who will be my helpers to (the work of Allah)? Said the Disciples: "We are Allah's helpers, we believe in Allah, and do thou

bear witness that we are Muslims."
(Q. 3:42-52)

Mary the mother of Jesus was unique, in that she gave birth to a son by a special miracle, without the intervention of the customary physical means. This of course does not mean that she was more than human. She had as much need to pray to Allah as anyone else. The Christian dogma, in all sects except the Unitarian, holds that Jesus was Allah and the son of Allah. The worship of Mary became the practice in the Roman Catholic Church, which calls Mary the mother of Allah. This seems to have been endorsed by the Council of Ephesus in 431, in the century before Prophet Mohammed (peace and blessings of Allah be upon him) was born to sweep away the corruptions of the Church of Christ. For **alamin** as meaning all nations.

The ministry of Jesus lasted only about three years, from 30 to 33 years of his age, when in the eyes of his enemies he was crucified. But the Gospel of luke (ii, 46) describes him as disputing with the doctors in the Temple at the age of 12, and even earlier, as a child, he was "Strong in spirit, filled with wisdom" (Luke ii, 40). Some apocryphal Gospels describe him as preaching from infancy.

Mary was addressed by angels, who gave her Allah's Message. In reply she speaks to Allah. In reply apparently an Angel again gives Allah's message.

The miracle of the clay bird is found in some of the apocrypha: Gospels; those of curing the blind and the lepers and raising the dead are in the canonical Gospels. The original Gospel did not have the various stories which were written afterwords by disciples.

The story of Jesus is told with special application to the time of the Prophet Mohammed (peace and blessings of Allah be upon him). Note the word `helpers' (*Ansar*) in this connection, and the reference to plotters in *surah* 3, *ayah* 54. It was the one religion --- the Religion of Allah, which was in essence the religion of Abraham, Moses and Jesus. The argument runs: why do ye then now make divisions and reject the living teacher? Islam is bowing to the Will of Allah. All who have faith should bow to the Will of Allah and be Muslim.

When Maryam saw Jibril in front of her as a young man of handsome form and beautiful countenance who had pierced the veil to reach her, she thought that he meant to do her harm. She was chaste and pure as Allah had brought her up. Therefore she sought refuge with Allah to protect her from him:

The holy Qur'an says:

"She said: "I seek refuge from thee to (Allah) Most Gracious: (come not near) if thou dost fear Allah.""

"He said: "Nay, I am only a Messenger from thy Lord (to announce) to thee the gift of a pure son.""

"She said: "How shall I have a son, seeing that no man has touched me, and I am not unchaste?""

"He said: "So (it will be) thy Lord saith,

"That is easy for Me: and (We wish) to appoint him as a Sign unto men, a Mercy from Us: it is matter (so decreed)""

Allah Almighty had destined her to be the mother of Prophet Jesus Christ, and now had come the time when this should be announced to her.

The mission of Jesus is announced in two ways:

1. He was to be a Sign to men; his wonderful birth and wonderful life were to turn an ungodly world back to Allah; and

2. His mission was similar to that of all Prophets of Allah. But the point here is that the Israelites, to whom Jesus was sent, were a hardened race, for which the message of Jesus was truly a gospel of Mercy.

For anything that Allah wishes to create, He says "Be", and it is. There is no interval between His decree and its accomplishment, except such as He imposes by His decree. Time may be only a projection of our own minds in this world of relativity.

Sometimes the angels take the form of ordinary people and contact certain people to inform them of what will make things easier for them and to expand their breasts to good deeds, praiseworthy actions and noble character.

Abu Hurairah (may Allah be pleased with him) reports that the Messenger of Allah (peace and blessings of Allah be upon him) said:

"A man visited a brother of his in another town and Allah delegated an angel to guard him on his way. When he came to him, the angel said, `Where are you going?' He said `I am going to visit a brother of mine in that town'. He said, `Do you have any property with him and you want to check on?' He said, `No, it is only that I love him for the sake of Allah.' He said, `I am the Messenger of Allah to you to tell you that Allah loves you as you love this man for His sake" (*Muslim*).

For Testing of Mankind

Abu Hurairah (may Allah be pleased with him) reports to have heard from the Messenger of Allah (peace and blessings of

Allah be upon him):

"Three of the tribes of Isra'il were respectively lepers, bald and blind. Allah Almighty wanted to put them to test and so He sent an angel to them. He came to the leper and said, 'What is the thing you would like best?' He said, 'A good complexion and fair skin and for the thing that I have which makes people find me unclean to be taken from me." He wiped him and his impurity left him and he gave him a good complexion. He said, 'What form of wealth do you like best?' He said, 'camels', and he gave him a pregnant she-camel, saying, 'May Allah bless you in it."

"Then he came to the bald man and said, 'What is the thing you would like best?" He said, 'A good head of hair and to have what people consider distasteful about me removed from me.' So he touched him and removed what he had and gave him a thick head of hair. He said, What form of wealth do you like best?' He said, 'Cattle'. So he gave him a pregnant cow and said, 'May Allah bless you in it.'

Then he went to the blind man and said, 'What is the thing you would like best?' He said, 'For Allah to return my sight to me so that I can see people.' He touched him and Allah returned his sight to him. He said, 'What form of wealth do you like best?' He said, 'Sheep'. So he gave him a pregnant sheep.

"These animals all gave birth and produced offspring. In time one had a valley full of camels, the other a valley full of cattle and the third a valley full of sheep.

"Then he (the angel) went to the leper, taking on the form that he himself had previously had, and said, 'I am a poor man who has lost his means on his journey. Today I can seek help from none but Allah and then you. I ask you, by the One Who gave you a good complexion and good skin and wealth, for a camel so that I can complete my journey.' He said, `I have many obligations.' He said, `I seem to recignize you. Were you not a leper that people found unclean, and poor and then Allah was generous to you?' He said, `I inherited this property, elder son from elder son.'He said, `If you are a liar in your claim, may Allah return you to your original state.'

He then went to the bald man taking on the form that he himself had previously had, and said to him the same as he had said to the other and he replied to him in the same way. He said, `If you are a liar, may Allah return you to your original state."

"Finally he went to the blind man and said, `I am a poor man who has lost his means on his journey. Today I can seek help from no one but Allah and then you. I ask you by the One Who returned your sight to you for a sheep so I can complete my journey.' He said, `I was blind and Allah restored my sight to me, so take what you want and leave what you want. By Allah I will not be hard on you about anything which you take for Allah Almighty. I will not be hard on you by refusing anything you ask of me or take.' He said, `Keep your wealth, you have been tested and Allah is pleased with you and angry with your companions."

The Angels of Death to Musa (p.b.u.h.)

Bukhari reports from Abu Hurairah (may Allah be pleased with him):

"The angel of death was sent to Musa (peace be upon him). When he came, Musa (p.b.u.h.) gave him a black eye so he returned to his Lord and said:

"You sent me to a slave who does not want to die."

Allah restored his eyes and said:

"Go back and tell him to put his hand on the back of an ox and he will live a year for every hair that his hand covers.

"O Lord, then what? Musa said.

"Then death', He said.

"Then let it be now.' Musa said.

Ibn Hajr said in *al-Fath:*

"His words, gave him a black eye' means that he hit him in the eye.

In another variant in *Muslim*, it has:

"The angel of death came to Musa and said, 'Answer to your Lord." Musa hit the Angel of Death in the eye and put it out.'

In a variant of Abu Hurairah (may Allah be pleased with him) in Ahmad Ibn Hanbal and at-Tibrani, we find:

"The angel of death used to come to people in a visible form. He went to Musa and he put out his eye."

Ibn Khuzayna said:

"Some of the heretics refuse to acknowledge this and say that if Musa recognised him, he did not take him seriously. If he did not recognize him, then how would he not have retaliation from him for putting out his eye? The answer is that Allah did not send the angel of Death to Musa desiring to take his soul at that moment, He sent him to him to test him. Musa punched the angel of Death because he thought that he was a human who had entered his house without his permission and did not know that he was the Angel of Death. The *Shari'ah* allows for the putting out of the eye of anyone who looks into a Muslim's house without permission. The Angels came to Ibrahim and to Lut in the human form and they did not recognize them at first. If Ibrahim had recognized them, he would not have offered them food. If Lut had recognized them he would not have feared for them from his people."

One of the people of knowledge said, "He hit him because he came to take his soul before giving him a choice since it is established that no Prophet is taken without being given a choice. This is why, when he gave him a choice the second time he submitted."

Ibn Hajr said:

"And Ibn Qutayba said, `Musa (p.b.u.h.) put out an eye which was imaginary symbolic and not a real eye. The meaning of Allah's restoring his eye is returning him to his true form. It is said that it was only his disguised form and that Allah restored him human eye to the Angel of Death so that he could return to Musa in a perfect form. That is the strongest interpretation and is the most reliable one."

Ibn Hajr then said, "There are lessons in the *hadith*: for instance, the angel can take on human form. There are also a number of other *hadiths* that show this."

Harut and Marut

Allah Almighty says :

الِتِيحْرَ وَمَاۤ أُنْزِلَ عَلَى الْمَلَكَيْنِ بِبَابِلَ هَارُوْتَ وَمَارُوْتَ وَمَايُعَلِّمَنِ مِنْ أَحَدٍ حَتَّى
يَقُوْلَاۤ إِنَّمَا نَحْنُ فِتْنَةٌ فَلَا كَفَرْ فَيَتَعَلَّمُوْنَ مِنْهُمَا مَايُفَرِّقُوْنَ بِهِ بَيْنَ الْمَرْءِ وَ
زَوْجِهِ

"Magic, and such things came down at Babylon to the angels
Harut and Marut. But neither of these taught anyone (such
things) without saying: we are only for trial; so do not
blaspheme. The learned from them the means to sow
discord between man and wife."

(Q. 2:102)

Harut and Marut lived in Babylon, a very ancient seat of
science, especially the science of astronomy. The period may be
supposed to be anywhere about the time when the ancient Eastern
Monarchies were strong and enlightened: probably even earlier, as
Babylon. Being good men, Harut and Marut of course dabbled in
nothing evil, and their hands were certainly clean of fraud. But
knowledge and the arts, if learned by evil men, can be applied to
evil uses. The evil ones, besides their fraudulent magic, also learnt
a little of this true science and applied it to evil uses. Harut and
Marut did not withhold knowledge, yet never taught anyone
without plainly warning them of the trial and temptation of knowledge in the hands of evil men. Being men of inside, they also saw
the blasphemy that might rise to the evil ones puffed up with science
and warned them against it. Knowledge is indeed a trial or
temptation: if we are warned, we know its danger: if Allah has
endowed us with free will, we must be free to choose between the
benefit and the danger.

Among the Jewish tradition in the Midrash (Jewish **Tafsirs**)
was a story of two angels who asked Allah's permission to come
down to earth but succumbed to temptations, and were hung up by
their feet at Babylon as punishment. Such stories about sinning

angels who were cast down to punishment were believed in by the early Christians also.

What the evil ones learnt from Harut and Marut they turned to evil. When mixed with fraud and deception, it appeared as charms and spells and love potions. They did nothing but cause discord between the sexes. But of course their power was limited to the extent to which Allah permitted the evil to work, for His grace protected all who sought His guidance and repented and returned to Him. But apart from the harm that these false pretenders might do to the others, the chief harm which they did was to their own souls. They sold themselves into slavery to the Evil.

> "There are many transmissions and extraordinary stories related from Ibn-Umar, Ibn Mas'ud, Ali, Ibn Abbas, Mujahid, K'ab, ar-Rabi and as-Suddi. Ibn Jarir at-Tabari relates them in his *Tafsir*, as do Ibn Mardawayh, al-Hakim, Ibn al-Mundir, Ibn Ali, Dunya, al-Bayhaqi, and al-Khatib in their *tafsirs* and books."

The basic picture gained from these accounts is that when people among the descendants of Adam fell into acts of the disobedience and disbelief in Allah, the angels in heaven said:

> "O Lord! you created this world for people to worship You and obey You and now they have committed acts of disobedience and rebellion and taken the lives which they had no right to take, consumed property unlawfully, stolen, committed fornication and drunk wine."

They began to curse them and did not find any excuse for them. It was said to them, "They are unaware", but they still did not excuse them.

One of the transmissions says that Allah said to them:

"If you had been in their place, you would have done the same as them."

"Glory be to you! That would not be something we would do", they said.

Another transmission has :

"They said, "No".

"Choose two angels from among yourselves whom I will command and forbid to disobey Me", it was said to them.

They chose Harut and Marut, who went down to earth and appetites were created in them. They were commanded to worship Allah and not to associate anything with Him and they were forbidden to take life without legal right to do so and to consume unlawful property, steal, commit fornication or drink wine. They remain in that way on earth for a considerable time, judging people by the Truth..

During that time, there was a woman whose beauty among people was like that of Venus among the stars. The two Angels tried to seduce her but she refused unless they would submit to authority and her religion. They asked her about her religion and she produced an idol for them. They said, "We cannot worship this", and they left and worshipped as Allah wished.

Then they came to her again and spoke humbly to her and tried once more to seduce her. Again she refused unless they took on her religion and worshipped the idol which she worshipped. They refused, and when she saw that they refused to worship her idol, she said to them, "Choose one of three things --- worship that idol, kill someone, or drink this wine." They said, "None of them is good but the least bad of the three is drinking the wine." So she gave them wine to drink until they were completely under its influence. A man passed by while they were doing this and they were afraid that he would give them away so they killed him

When the state of intoxication left them, they realised what a terrible mistake they had made and tried to ascend back up to heaven but they were unable to do so. Then the veil between them and the inhabitants of the heavens was removed. The angels looked at the wrong actions they had done and realised that those who are unaware are lacking in fear. After that they began to ask forgiveness for the people of the earth.

After they had committed this error, the two Angels were told to choose between the punishmetn of this world which comes to an end, whereas the punishment of the next world lasts for ever." So they chose the punishment of this world and they were sent to Babel where they were punished by being suspended upside down by their feet.

In one transmission, it says that they taught the woman the word by which she could ascend to heaven and she ascended and Allah transformed her and she became the star known as Venus!

All this is part of the myths and lies of the tribe of Isra'il and is not corroborated either by intellect or transmission or **Shari'ah.** Some of the transmitters of this false fiction even go so far as to ascribe its transmission to some of the Companions and Followers but in doing so they enter the arena of sin and shameful crime and at the same time connect this lie to the Prophet (peace and blessings of Allah be upon him) by taking it back to him. Glory be to You, my Lord, above and beyond this terrible lie.'

Imam Abu Faraj Ibn al-Jawzi gave a judgement about this story, and ash-Shihab al-Iraqi writes that anyone who believes that Harut and Marut were two angels who are bing punished for their sin has disbelieved in Allah Almighty.

Qadi Iyad said in **ash-shifa'**, "what is said in the reports and commentaries about the story of Harut and Marut does not relate anything, either sound or weak, from the Messenger of Allah (peace and blessings of Allah upon him) himself, and there is nothing which is taken by analogy."

A similar judgement was made by Ibn Kathir in respect of tracing the material in this story back to the Prophet.

As for what does not go back to the Prophet it is clear that it originates in the transmission of the Jewish material taken from Ka'b and others. It is the heretics of the people of the Book who connected them to Islam. Thus accurate commentators, who are skillful in recognising the source of the *deen*, refute them. Their intellects refuse to accept these myths, as do those of others such as Imam ar-Razi, Abu Hayyan, Abus Sa`ud, al-Alusi, and others.

Another of these transmissions has Allah saying to them, "If I tested you in the same way as I tested the tribe of Adam, you would also disobey Me." They said, "If you were to do that, O Lord, we would certainly not disobey you,' "To refute the words of Allah constitutes disbelief. Any human being who possesses knowledge of Allah and His attirbute is free of that let alone the angels. And how could a corrupt woman ascend to heaven and become a radiant star.'What is that star which they claim to be Venus and at the same time a woman? She would have had to have been transformed on the day Allah created the heavens and the earth!

These myths are not corroborated either by sound transmission or sound reason. Not only that but they differ from what has come clear certainly through the knowledge of modern scientists. I do not understand what our position is supposed to be in respect of the astronomers and cosmologists since we do not repudiate these myths and are either silent about them or support them!

But these tales and myths are Israeli in nature and substance and have been twisted from their correct meaning. Allah Almighty says in the Qur'an:

وَاتَّبَعُوا مَا تَتْلُوا الشَّيَاطِينُ عَلَى مُلْكِ سُلَيْمَنَ ۖ وَمَا كَفَرَ سُلَيْمَنُ وَلَكِنَّ الشَّيَاطِينَ كَفَرُوا يُعَلِّمُونَ النَّاسَ السِّحْرَ وَمَا أُنْزِلَ عَلَى الْمَلَكَيْنِ بِبَابِلَ هَارُوتَ وَمَارُوتَ وَمَا يُعَلِّمَنِ مِنْ أَحَدٍ حَتَّى يَقُولَا إِنَّمَا نَحْنُ فِتْنَةٌ فَلَا تَكْفُرْ ۖ فَيَتَعَلَّمُونَ مِنْهُمَا مَا يُفَرِّقُونَ بِهِ بَيْنَ الْمَرْءِ وَزَوْجِهِ ۚ وَمَا هُمْ بِضَارِّينَ بِهِ مِنْ أَحَدٍ إِلَّا بِإِذْنِ اللَّهِ ۚ وَيَتَعَلَّمُونَ مَا يَضُرُّهُمْ وَلَا يَنْفَعُهُمْ ۚ وَلَقَدْ عَلِمُوا لَمَنِ اشْتَرَاهُ مَا لَهُ فِي الْآخِرَةِ مِنْ خَلَاقٍ ۚ وَلَبِئْسَ مَا شَرَوْا بِهِ أَنْفُسَهُمْ ۚ لَوْ كَانُوا يَعْلَمُونَ

"They followed what the Satans recited over Solomon's kingdom. Solomon did not disbelieve but Satans disbelieved, teaching men magic, and such things as came down at Babylon to the angels Harut and Marut. But neither of these taught anyone (such things) without saying: "We are only for trial; so do not blaspheme." They learned from them the means to sow discord between man and wife. But they could not thus harm anyone except by Allah's permission. And they learned what harmed them, not what profited them. And they knew that the buyers of magic would have no share in the happiness of the Hereafter. and vile was the price for which they did sell their souls, if they but knew!"

(Q. 2:102)

There is nothing in this *ayah* which gives any indication whatsoever of this disreputable story. That was not the reason for the sending down of the ayah. The reason was that the Satans in that distant time used to drop in the heavens and then add lies to what they had heard, which they would then pass on to the soothsayers and rabbis of the Jews, They, in turn, would record these fabrications in the books they read and taught to other people.

This spread in the time of Sulayman (Solomon), (peace be upon him) to the point that people said: "This is the science of Sulayman, and the kingdom of Sulayman was only made possible by it. It was by this means that he subjugated men and jinn and the wind which ran at his command."

This is one of the lies the Jews told about the Prophets. Allah Almighty accused them of lying when he says·

"**Sulayman did not reject but the satans did reject and taught people sorcery**."

Then He adds to that, "**and what had been sent down to the two angels in Babylon, Harut and Marut.**" By "**What had been sent down**" He means the science of magic, which was sent down so that they could teach it to people and warn them against it. The reason the two of them were sent down was to teach people what magic was so that they would then know the difference between magic and Prophethood, and therefore that Sulayman was not a magician. It was to ensure a complete understanding.

They did not, in any case, teach anyone magic until they had first cautioned him saying to him, "We are merely a temptation and a trial and a test, so do not become unbelievers by teaching it and using it." Part of the point of the teaching was to warn people against it and to teach them the difference between it and prophethood and prophetic miracles. There is nothing wrong with this. Indeed, if something is desirable and meritorious there is real need for it.

However, people did not take their advice and they would use magic to separate a man from his wife. That was by the permission and Will of Allah. The *ayah* indicates that it is permitted to teach people magic in order to warn people against succumbing to it and acting by it and there is no sin in that. It is also permissible to teach it to eliminate any resemblance between it and true miracles and prophethood and there is no sin in that. What is unlawful and a sin is to teach it or learn it in order to use it. This point is well illustrated by the sayings: "I learned evil not for evil's sake, but in order to be safe from it." And also: "People who do not recognise evil, fall into it."

When the Messenger of Allah (peace and blessings of Allah be upon him) came to the Jews, they knew that he was the Propet, the good news of whom had been given in Torah, and they used to pray for his health agianst the idol-worshippers before he was born and sent. But then when he did come to them they would not acknowledge him and rejected him. They cast their book, the Torah, and the Book of Allah, the Qur'an, behind their backs.

Allah Almighty indicates that they should follow the clear truth but they preferred to follow the magic they had inherited form their fathers and which the Satans had taught them, even though it was obligatory for them to reject magic and caution people against its evil. That was what the two angels, Harut and Marut, did: warn people against the evils of magic and against using it.

This is the sound *tafsir* of the *ayah*, not what stupid falsifiers claim. Through this understanding, harmony between the passages is obtained and the true value of the *ayah* is recalled. One cannot imagine how people can see any connection between the Jewish material they have related and the words of the Almighty:

"They taught no one until they had told him, `We are merely a trial and a temptation, so do not reject."

The extraordinary thing is that Imam Ibn Jarir talked about these things in his commentary of the *ayah* and apparently had no hesitation in doing so

A Significant Dream

Bukhari reports Samura bin Jundub.(may Allah by pleased with him) to have said:

"The Messenger of Allah (Peace and Blessings of Allah be upon him) would often say to his companions: `Who among you had a dream last night?'

Then anyone who Allah willed would recount his dream. One morning he said to us, `During the night two men came to me and said to me, "come on!" So I went with them. We came upon a man who was lying on his back while another man was standing over with a stone which he dropped on to his head and crushed it. Then the stone rolled away from him and he went after the stone to retrieve it. When he returned to him, his head was whole again and head became as it had been in the first place. So he went back and hit him as he had done the first time. I said to them, "Glory be to Allah! Who are these two?"

"They said, "Go on! Go on!" We went on and came to a man lying on his back and there was another man standing over him with an iron hook. He went to one side of his face and gashed upon the side of his mouth until it reached the back of his neck and then his nostril to the back of his neck and his eye to the back of his neck. Then he moved to the other side and did the same things as he had done to the first side, the first side had become whole again. Then he did the same thing all over again. "He said, "I said, "Glory be to Allah!

Who are these two?"

"They said to me, "Go on! Go on!" and we went on until we came upon something like an oven. In it was a babble and shouting. We looked down into it and it contained naked men and women. The flames leapt up at them from underneath, and when those flames reached them, they cried out. I said, "Who are they?"

"They said, "Go on! Go on!" and we went on until we came to a river, red like blood. In the river there was a man swimming and on the bank of the river was a man who had, many stones with him. When that swimmer swam and reached the bank one who had gathered the stones, forced his mouth open and made him swallow a stone. Then he would begin to swim and would come back to him again. Whenever he came back to him, he forced open his mouth and made him swallow a stone. I said to them, "Who are these two?"

"They said to me, "Go on! Go on!" and we went on until we came to a man with the most repulsive appearance you have ever seen. He was at a fire which he was kindling and which he was running around. I said to them, "Who is this?"

"They said to me "Go on! Go on!" and went on until we came to a green meadow with every type of spring flower in it. There was, in the middle of the meadow, a man so tall that I could scarcely see his head, so high it was in the sky. Around the man were the greatest number of children I have ever seen. I said, "Who is this? Who are those?"

"They said to me "Go on! Go on!" and we went on until we reached a huge tree and I have never seen any tree bigge or more beautiful than this. They said to me. "Climb it." We climbed it and came to the door of the city and asked for it to be opened and it was opened for us and we entered it. We were met by men half of whose physique was the most beautiful you have ever seen and the other half was the ugliest you have ever seen. The two said to them. "Go and plunge into that river." There was a wide river flowing there whose water was pure white. They went and jumped into it and when they returned to us, that evil had left them and they had the most beautiful form."

He said, ' They said to me, "This is the Garden of Eden, and that is your place, "I raised my eyes upwards and there was a castle like a white cloud. They said to me, "This is your place." I said to them, "May Allah bless you, let me enter it." They said, "No, not now But you will enter it."

"I said to them, "This night I have seen marvels, but what are these things which I have seen?" They said to me, "We will tell you. The first man you came to whose head was being crushed with the stone is a man who memorised the Qur'an and then abondoned it and slept through obligatory prayers.

As for the man you came to whose jaw was split to his neck, whose nostrils to his neck and whose eyes to his neck, he was a man who went from his house and told lies which spread everywhere. As for the naked men and women who were in something like an oven, they were adulterers. The man you came to who was swimming in the river and being made to swallow stones used to consume usury. The man kindling fire and runngin around it, was Malik, the custodian of Hell. The tall man in the meadow was Ibrahim.' The children who were around him are all those who were born and died in the natural state."

"Some of the Muslims asked, "Messenger of Allah, the

children of the idol-worshippers as well?' The Messenger of Allah (peace and blessings of Allah be upon him) said, `The children of the idol-worshippers as well. As for the people who were half beautiful and half ugly, they are people who mixed righteous actions with evil actions. Allah pardoned them."

The meanings of the expressions in this **hadith** are explained in the **Fath al-Barr**. In his words (peace and blessings of Allah be upon him): "During the night two men came to me." The two men are, as has come into another vairant with Jibril bin Hazim, Jibril and Mika'il.

About his words, "They came to me", Ibn Jubayr says that it means they woke him up. It is possible that he saw in a dream that they woke him up and he saw what he saw in the dream and described it after he was awake, and his dream was like being awake. However what he saw was a metaphor whose difficulty of interpretation indicated that it was a dream.

Regardig his words, "I went with them, "Jarir adds in this variant "to the Holy Land", and with *Ahmad* we find, "to an open land." The *hadith* of Ali has, "They took me to heaven."

His, words, "We came to a man who was lying on his back while another man was standing over him with a stone, "means thrown unto his back. In Ali's *hadith* we find, "I passed by an angel in front of whom was a human being. The angel had a stone in his hand with which he was beating the man's head."

His word, "crushed it" means to shatter something hollow.

His words, "and the stone rolled away" means went from a higher place to a lower one and it is the word used for something rolling down by itself.

His words, "When he returned to him, his head was whole again," Ahmad has here, "His head returned as it had been."

His words, "he gashed open side of his mouth until it reached the back of his neck" means to split it in two. The shida is the corner of the mouth. Ibn al-Arabi said, `to gash open the corner of the mouth of the liar is to put the punishment in the site of the act of disobedience. It is on this basis that punishment occurs in the Next World, contrary to the way things happen in this world."

His words, "We came upon something like an oven", reads in the variant of Mohammed bin J'afar. "Built like the structure of an oven." and Jarr adds, "Its top was narrow and its bottom wide, and there was a fire kindled under it."

His words, "they cried out" means they raised their voices in such a way that they were muddled up together.

His words, "Which he was kindling" means setting fire to It says in at-Tahdhib, "He kindled the fire with wood, he collected together for the fire scattered firewood. Ibn al-Arabi says that it means poking the fire.

About the words, "We came to a green meadow", I said that this refers to a meadow which is covered in green.

Instead of his words, "With every type of spring flower in it", another variant has, "all the flowers of spring."

His words, "plunge into that river" means to be immersed in it in order to wash away that attribue by this pure water.

His words, "that evil had left them" means the ugly side became the same as the beautiful side.

His words, "then abandoned it" is that abandoning the Qur'an after memorising it is a terrible cirme because he imagines that he sees in it something that obliges him to abandon it. When he abandons the noblest things, which is the Qur'an he is punished in the noblest of limbs, which is the head.

His words, "and slept through the obligatory prayers" means that he was lazy about performing them in their correct times, and Allah has threatened those people in His words:

فَوَيْلٌ لِلْمُصَلِّينَ ۝ الَّذِينَ هُمْ عَنْ صَلَاتِهِمْ سَاهُونَ

"Woe to those that pray and are heedless in their prayers.
(Q. 107:4-5)

His words, "they were adulterers" shows that nakedness is appropriate for them since they deserve to be disgraced because their custom was to conceal themselves in private. Therefore they are punished by exposure. The wisdom in bringing the punishment from underneath them is that their crime was from their lower limbs.

About his words, "he used to consume usury", Ibn Hubayra said that the one who consumes usury is punished by swimming in the red river and being made to swallow stones becaue the basis of usury is to deal in gold ad gold is red. As for the Angel making him swallow stones, it indicates that nothing satisfied him. It is the same with usury. The one who uses it imagines that his wealth will increase but Allah wipes it out from behind him.

"The custodian of Hell" has a disagreeable appearance because that increases the punishment for the people of the Fire.

In the *hadith* of Abu Umama we find, "then we went on and there were men and women of the ugliest appearance and the foulest smell, like that of sewers. I said, `Who are these? he said, `those are dead of unbelievers.' Then we went on and there were some men asleep under the shadow of a tree. I said, `Who are these? He said, `those are the Muslim dead.' Then we went on and there were some men who had the most handsome faces and most fragrant perfume and I said, `Who are these?' He said, those are the truthful, the martyrs and the righteous."

Ibn Hajr said that this *hadith* contains many salutary lessons. Secrets make themselves known to people both in the waking and sleeping states in various ways. It also shows that some rebels are between the worlds. There is the warning against sleeping through the prescribed prayers, against someone who has memorised Qur'an abondoning it, and against fornication, consuming usury and delibrately lying. It shows that those who have a palace in the Garden do not reside in it while in this world, but that happens only after death, even in the case of Prophets and martyrs.

Their homes in the Garden are the highest homes, but that does not mean that they have a higher degree than Ibrahim, (peace be upon him) since it is probable that he is residing in that place only on account of his tutelage of those children. His station is a station which is higher than that of the martyrs. This was already shown in the *hadith* of the Night Journey when the Prophet saw Adam in the lowest heaven. He was in that place in order to see the souls of his sons among the people of good and the people of evil, and to laugh and weep accrodingly, although his station is in fact in **Illiyin**. On the Day of Rising, all people will be residing in their proper place and on that day Allah will pardon all those good or evil actions which are equal in weight. O Allah! Pardon us by Your mercy, O Most Merciful the Merciful!

This *hadith* also shows the importance of dreams in general by the mere fact that the Prophet wishes about them, the excellence of dream interpretation, and the preference of doing it after the *Fajr* prayer because that is the time when the mind is most collected.

Angels Praying for Righteous Actions

The holy Qur'an speaks of the descent of the angels to the earth on the Night of the Power durig month of Ramadan. That is the night on which the Qur'an first came down to Mohammed (peace and blessings of Allah be upon him), when the Qur'an descended from the (*Lauh-e-Mahfooz-Preserved Tablet*) down to the lowest heaven and heralded the descent of revelation on the Seal of the Prophets (peace and blessings of Allah be upon him). This is why the angels descend during it, and Jibril the Trustworthy descends during it. He is the one meant by the word "Spirit" in Allah's words:

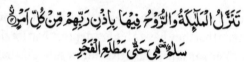

"On it the angels and the Spirit descend, by the leave of their Lord, upon every command. Peace it is, until the rising dawn."   (Q. 97:4-5)

They do not descend on their ow initiative, but only in obedience to divine authority, "the leave of their Lord."

Al-Qurtubi says in his **tafsir** of this *ayah*: "On it the angels, and the Spirit descend, by the leave of their Lord, upon every command", i.e. they descend from every heaven and from the Lot Tree of the Furthest Limit and the dwelling -- place of Jibril in the centre of it. They descend to the earth and give security to the people there making supplication until the moment of the rising of the dawn. That is the explanation of His words. "On it the angels and the Spirit descend, i.e., Jibril (peace be upon him), "by the leave of their Lord", at His **command**, "upon every command, i.e., every command which Allah decrees and decides from that year to the next. Ibn Abbas said that.|

Anas said, "On the Night of Power, Jibril (peace be upon him) descends with a group of angels to pray and to greet every slave, standing or sitting, who is remembering Allah Almighty."

His words, "**Peace it is, untill the rising of dawn**" means that the Night of Power is peace and all good with no evil in it. `**Untill the rising of dawn**' is untill dawn breaks.

Ash-Shabi said, "It is the greeting of the angels to the people of the Mosque from the time the sun disappears until the dawn rises. They pass by every believer and say, `peace be upon you O believer!"

Recitation of the Qur'an

Bukhari transmits with his *isnad* from Usayd bin Hurayr (may Allah be pleased with him) who said that once while he was reciting *Surah* al-Baqarah at night, with his horse tethered beside him, it suddenly became very agitated. When he stopped reciting, the horse calmed down. When he started to recite again, the horse once again began agitated. Then he stopped reciting and the horse calmed down again. Then he recited and the horse became agitated so he stopped. His son Yahya was close to the horse and he was afraid that it might trample on him.

When he pulled the boy away and looked up to the sky, he could not see it. In the morning, he told the Prophet (peace and blessings of Allah be upon him) who said:

"Recite, Ibn Hurayr! Recite, Ibn Hurayr!" He said, "Messenger of Allah, I was afraid that the horse would trample on Yahya since he was near to it. I looked up and went to him. When I looked at the sky, there was something in it like a cloud containing something like lamps. So I left in order not to see it." He said, "Do you know what that was?" He said, "No". He said, "That was the angel who came near on account of your voice if you had continued to recite, in the morning the people could have looked at it and it would not have disappeared from them."

"The horse became agitated" means it jumped about.

The words, "He pulled the boy away." Means he dragged him from the place where he was fearing that the horse would trample on him.

About the words, "He looked up to the sky and he could not see it", Ibn Hajr says that this transmission is abridged. Aby Ubayd related it in full saying, "he looked up to the sky and there was something in it like a cloud containing somethig like lamps. It rose up into the sky so that he could not see it."

The words of the Prophet (peace and blessings of Allah be upon him), "Recite, Ibn Hurayr!" means that he should have continued reciting. It was not a command to recite at the moment of the conversation. It is as if the Prophet was visualising the situation and was present with him when he saw what he saw. It is as if he were saying: "Continue your recitation, so that the blessings continues with you by the descent of the Angels and their listening to your recitation." So Usayd understood that and he replied giving an excuse for having curtailed his recitation, consisting of his words, "I was afraid it would trample on Yahya", i.e. I feared that if I continued reciting, the horse would trample on my son.

His words, "who came near" has, in the variant of Ibrahim bin Sa d, the additional phrase, "to listen to you", and in the variant of Ibn Ka'b we find, "Usayd had a good voice." This addition indicates the reason why the angels were listening to his recitation.

An-Nawawi said, "This *hadith* shows that it is permissible for individuals of the community to see the angels." Ibn Hajr said, "This interpretation is sound, but it is limited, for instance, to the righteous, and to people with good voices."

He said tht the *hadith* shows the excellecne of recitation and the fact that it is a reason form the descent of mercy and the presence of the angels.

Muslim transmits in his *Sahih* from Abu Hurairah (may Allah be pleased with him) who said that the Messenger of Allah (peace and blessings of Allah be upon him), said:

> "No people gather in any of the houses of Allah to recite the Book of Allah and to study it between them but that the *Sakina* descends on them and mercy covers them and the angels surrounded them and Allah remembers them to those in His presence."

In the two *Sahih* collections of *al-Bukhari* and *Muslim*, Abu Hurairah (may Allah be pleased with him) said that the Prophet (peace and blessings of Allah be upon him), said:

> "Allah the Blessed and Exalted, has angels who travel the highways seeking out the people of *dhikr*. When they find people remembering Allah Almighty, they call out to one another: `Come to what you hunger for!' and they enfold them with their wings stretchings up to the lowest heaven."

Ahmad transmitted in his *Musnad* as did Abu Ya`la and at-Tibrani in **al-Awsat** that Anas (may Allah be pleased with him) said that the Messenger of Allah (peace and blessings of Allah be upon him) said:

> "No people sit to remember Allah but that a caller from heaven calls out to them, `Arise forgiven."

Muslim, at-Tirmidhi and *an-Nasa'i* transmit from the **hadith** of Mu'awiya:

> "The Messenger of Allah (peace and blessings of Allah be upon him) went out to a circle of his Companions and said:
>
> What is it that has caused you to sit together?'
>
> `We sat down to remember Allah and praise him for He has guided us to Islam and been gracious to us', they said,
>
> `By Allah, is that the only thing that made you sit together?' he said.
>
> `By Allah, we sat down for that reason alone', they said.
>
> I did not make you swear out of any suspicion of you, but Jirbil came to me and reported to me that Allah Almighty is boasting about you to the angels", he said.

This boasting on the part of Allah Almighty is an indication of the nobility of *dhikr* in His sight and His love of it and that it has merit over other actions. *Dhikr* makes Allah Almighty and His angels to pray for those who do it. Whoever has Allah Almighty and his angels pray for him has complete success and total victory. Allah Almighty says:

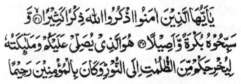

"O ye who believe! Remember Allah with much remembrance; and glorify Him morning and evening. He it is Who sends blessings on you, as do His angels, that he may bring you out from the depths of Darkness into Light and He is full of Mercy to the Believers.   (Q. 33:41-43)

Blessings: Good wishes and mercies. Allah wishes well to all the creatures, and His angels carry out His work, for their will is in all thing His Will. His chief and everlasting blessings is that He gives us knowledge of the spiritual world, and helps us towards its attainment.

His Mercies are for all His creatures, but for those who believe and trust in Him, there are special mercies, "a generous Reward" as in the next verse.

The Prophet was sent by Allah in five capacitites. Three are mentioned in this verse and the other two in the verse following:

1) He comes as a **witness** to all men about all spiritual truths which had been obscured by ignorance or superstition or by the dust of sectarian controversy. He did not come to establish a new religion or sect. He came to teach Religion. He is also a witness to Allah about men's doing and how they recieve Allah's Message.

2) He comes as a bearer of the **Glad Tidings** of the Mercy of Allah. No matter how far men may have transgressed, they have hope if they believe, repent and live a good life.

3) He also comes as a **Warner** to those who, are heedless. This life will not last. There is a Future Life, and that is all important.

Allah Almighty further says :

وَدَاعِيَّالَى اللهِ بِاِذْنِهِ وَسِرَاجًامُّنِيْرًا

"And as one who invites to Allah's (Grace) by His leave, and as a Lamp spreading Light."   (Q. 33:46)

The two other capacities in which the Prophet was sent are here specified:

4) He comes as one who has a right to invite all men to repentance and the forgiveness of sins: but he does this, not of his own authority, but by the permission and authority given to him by Allah. This is said lest people may deify the Prophet as they did with other Prophets before him. The personal responsibility of each individual remains, but the Prophet can lead him on the Right and help him.

5) The Prohet also comes as **Light** or a lamp **(Siraj)** to illuminate the whole world. At a number of places the same word **(Siraj)** is used for the sun. The comparison is apt. When the sun appears, all the lesser lights pale before its light. And the message of Islam, i.e., of the Universal Religion, is to diffuse **Light** everywhere.

The light of Islam is the Biggest Bounty possible and they truly understand it, they should glory in it

Ibn al-Qayyim said:

"This prayer from the Almighty and His angels is the cause of people comimg out the darkness to the light. When they receive the prayer from Allah Almighty and His angels and they are brought out of the darkness to the light, what good do they not obtain and what evil is not repelled from them! O alas for those who are heedless of their Lord! What blessing and bounty they are deprived of!"

Teaching Righteousness

At-Tibrani and at-Tirmidhi transmitted with sound *isnad* from Abu Umama (may Allah be pleased with him) that the Messenger of Allah (peace and blessings of Allah be upon him) said:

"Allah and His angels, and even the ant in its stone and the fish in the sea, pray for the one who teaches the people good.

In another variant:

"A man of knowledge has those in the heavens and the earth, even the fish in the sea, ask for his forgiveness."

Ibn Rajab al-Hanbi said:

"Some scholars have mentioned that the secret of animals of the earth asking for forgiveness for men of knowledge is that the men of knowledge command people to treat all creatures well and to kill those animals it is permitted to kill or slaughter properly. Therefore their good influence extends to all animals and that is why they ask forgiveness for them.

Another meaning is also evident from it, and that is that all animals obey Allah Almighty willingly, and glorify Him without disobeying. Therefore all creation which obeys Allah also loves the people who obey Him. So how much more so it is in the case of someone who truly knows Allah, His rights and the obedience due to Him! If anyone has this quality, Allah loves him and purifies him and praises him and commands His slaves among the people of the heavens and the earth and all creatures to love him and pray for him. That is their prayer on him, and He placed love for him in the hearts of His believing slaves.."

Seeking Useful Knowledge

Ahmad transmitted in his **Musnad** as did the people of the **Sunan** that Abu Darda (may Allah be pleased with him) said:

"I heard the Messenger of Allah (peace and blessings of Allah be upon him) say:

"Allah will make the path to the Garden easy for anyone who

travels a path in search of knowledge. Angels spread their wings for the seeker of knowledge out of pleasure for what he is doing. Everyone in the heavens and everyone in the earth asks forgiveness for a man of knowledge, even the fish in the water. The superiority of the man of knowledge to the man of worship is like the superiority of the moon to all the planets. The men of knowledge are the heirs of the Prophets. The Prophets bequeath neither dinar nor dirham; they bequeath knowledge. Whoever takes it has taken an ample portion."

Praying for the Visitors of the Masjid

In the **Sahih** of Muslim we find:

"The angels pray on the one who comes to the Masjid saying, 'O Allah, bless him! O Allah, show mercy to him! as long as he does no harm and does not break *wudu*.'"

Abu Hurairah (may Allah be pleased with him) said that the Messenger of Allah (peace and blessings of Allah be upon him) said:

"The group prayer is twenty-five degrees higher than the prayer in your place of business. Anyone who does **wudu** and goes to the Masjid with no other object then to do the prayer, Allah will raise him up a degree with every step he takes, and a wrong action will fall away from him. When he prays, the angels pray for him all the time he is in his place of saying:

'O Allah! Forgive him! O Allah! Show mercy to him!' one of you is in the prayer as long as he is waiting for the prayer."

In one variant,

"O Allah, forgive him! O Allah, turn to him as long as he does no harm in it and does not break **wudu** in it."

Al-Bukhari, Muslim, Abu Dawud, at-Tirmidhi and Malik related it.

The meaning of "as long as he does no harm in it" is as long as he does not harm any of those praying by word or deed.

The meaning of "as long as he does not break **wudu**" is as long as wind issues from him. This is why it recommended for a Muslim to do **wudu** whenever he breaks it so that he obtains the prayer of the angels on himself.

Ibn Hajr said that this *hadith* demonstrates the virtues of the prayer over other actions by mentioning the prayer of the angels on him and their prayer for mercy, forgiveness and *tauba* for him. It also demonstrates the excellence of the righteous people over the angels because they obtain degrees through their worship while the angels are occupied with asking forgiveness and supplication for them."

Praying in the First Row

Abu Dawud and Ibn Majah and the **Musnad** of Ahmad all have that al-Bara (may Allah be pleased with him) said:

"Allah and his angels pray in the first row."

In the **isnad** of at-Tirmidhi:

"Allah and His angels pray on the front row."

Al-Bukhari transmitted that Abu Hurairah said that the Messenger of Allah (peace and blessings of Allah be upon him) said:

"If people knew what there was in doing **Dhuhr** prayer at

its time, they would raise each other to it and if they knew what there was in the prayers of **Isha** and **Fajr**, they would come to them even if they had to crawl. If they knew what there was in the call to prayer and the first row, they would draw lots for it."

Ibn Hajr said·

"What is meant by the first row is the row immediately behind the Imam and it is the first complete row behind the Imam, not one that has any gaps in it. Scholars say that this encouragement for people to join the first row is in order for them to hasten to discharge their responsibility, to hurry to enter the mosque (Masjid), to be near the Imam and to listen to his recitation and learn from it and to be inspired by it and convey what he says, to be safe from someone else passing in front of him, to feel safe from seeing anyone in front of him, and for the place of his prostration to be safe from the coat tails of anybody praying in front."

On Jum'a Day

Al-Bukhari reports from Abu Hurairah (may Allah be pleased with him) that the Messenger of Allah (peace and blessings of Allah be upon him) said:

"On the day of Jum'a, the angels stand at the door of the Mosque and write down the first to come and then those who follow. When the Imam comes out, they roll up their scrolls and listen to the reminder."

Ibn Hajr said in the **Fath** and Abu Nu'aym transmitted it as **marfu** in al-Hilya with the expression:

"On the day of **Jum'a** Allah sends angels with scrolls of light and pens of light."

This indicates that the angels mentioned are not guardian angels. What is meant by the rolling up of the scrolls in to roll up the scrolls of the benefits connected with going early to Jum'a as opposed to any other prayer; not those of listening to the Khutba, catching the prayer, **dhikr**, supplication, humility and other such things. The guardian angels naturally write these things down. In the variant of Ibn ` Uyayna from az-Zuhri at the end of this **hadith** in Ibn Majah we find "anyone coming after that, comes merely for the sake of the prayer."

The Fajr and the Asr Prayers in Masjid

Abu Hurairah (may Allah be pleased with him) reports that the Messenger of Allah (peace and blessings of Allah be upon him) said:

"There are angels who take turns in being with you in the night and other angels in the day, and they meet together at the prayers of Fajr and Asr. Then the ones who were with you during the night ascend and Allah ask them--although he knows better than they do--'How were My slaves when you left them?'They say,'When we left them they were praying and when we came to them they were praying.'"

Al-Bukhari, Muslim, an-Nasa'i and Ibn Khuzayma related about his words, "There are angels who take turns in being with you", Ibn Hajr said, "It is said that they are the guardian angels.

Abu-Qurtubi said:

"I think that the most evident view is that it is other than them. This view is strengthened by the fact that it is not transmitted that the guardian angels ever leave the slave nor

that the guardian angels of the night are not the same as the
guardian angels of the day."

`Iyad said:

"The wisdom of them meeting at these two prayers is part of
Allah's kindness to His slaves and His generosity to them
since He made the angels meet at a time when His slaves are
in a state of obediencee so that they can give the best
testimony on their behalf.'

Ibn Hajr said in the **Fath**, "The **hadith** contains an indication
of the immense importance if these two prays since the two groups
meet during them while there is only one group present during the
other prayers. This indicates the nobility of the two times mentioned. It
is related that provision is allocated after the Fajr prayer and that
actions ascend at the end of the day. So whoever is engaged in an
act of obedience at that time is blessed both in his provision and in
his actions, and Allah knows best. It also shows that this community
is honoured above others and means therefore that its Prophet is
honoured above all other Prophets. It informs us of the love of
Allah's angels for us so that our love for them is increased and we
draw near to Allah by that. There are other salutory lessons, and
Allah knows them best."

Sadaqa and Good Spending

Al-Bukhari transmitted, with hi. *nad* from Abu Hurairah
(may Allah be pleased with him) that the Prophet of Allah (peace
and blessings of Allah be upon him) said:

"There is no day which dawns cn the slaves of Allah without
two angels descending and one often saying:

O Allah, refund those who gives money,' and the other

saying, `O Allah ruin those who withhold it."

There is also the **hadith** of Abu Darda' who said that the Messenger of Allah (peace and blessings of Allah be upon him) said:

"There is no day on which the sun rises but that it is accompanied by two angels who call out -- and all of Allah's creations hear it except for men and jinn -- `O people! Hasten to your Lord. What is little and adequate is better than what is abundant, and headless.' And the sun does not set but that it is accompanied by two angels who call out and one of them says.

`O Allah, ruin those, who withhold it."

An-Nawawi says that praiseworthy spending is what is spent in acts of obedience and on behalf of your family and guests and in voluntary acts of charity.

Al-Qurtubi said that this includes both obligatory and recommended giving, but that those who withhold from recommended giving do not merit this supplication nor those dominated by miserliness to the extent that they are not happy about giving out what is due from them, even if they do it.

On Performing Hajj

At-Tabarani and others transmitted from the *hadith* of Abu Hurairah (may Allah be pleased with him) who said:

"When a man sets on for **Hajj** with wholesome provision, places his foot in the stirrup and calls out, `At your service O Allah', then a caller from the heaven calls out, `At your service and obedience! Your provision is lawful and your mount is lawful and your **Hajj** is accepted and unencumbered. When a man sets out with unwholesome provision and puts his foot in the stirrup and says, `At your service O Allah', then a caller from the heaven calls out, `You have no service or obedience! Your provision is unlawful and your mount is unlawful, and your **Hajj** is not accepted."

Muslim transmitted in his **Sahih** from `Ayesha'(may Allah be pleased with her) that the Prophet of Allah (peace and blessings of Allah be upon him) said:

"There is no day on which Allah Almighty more frequently frees His slaves from the Fire than the Day of *Arafa* and He draws near and boasts of them to the angels and asks, `What do these people want?"

Jabir (may Allah be pleased with him) reports that the Prophet of Allah (peace and blessings of Allah be upon him) said:

"There is no day better with Allah Almighty than the Day of *Arafa*. On it Allah Almighty descends to the lowest heaven to boast of the people of the earth to the people of heaven and He says:

"Look at My slaves, dishevelled, dusty, and without shade. They have come through every deep revine, hoping for My mercy and they will not see my punishment, 'So there is no day when mor _ people are set free from the Fire than on the Day of Arafa'.

Martyrdom for Allah

Jabir bin Abdullah (may Allah be pleased with him) reports:

"When my father was killed, I began to lift the cloth from his face, weeping, but they stopped me. The Prophet of Allah (peace and blessings of Allah be upon him) did not stop me. My aunt Fatima began to weep and the Prophet (peace and blessings of Allah be upon him) said:

"It does not matter whether you weep or do not weep. The angels are shading him with their wings until you remove it.

Al-Bukhari transmitted it and al-Bukhari has a chapter entitled, "The chapter of the Angels shading the Martyr."

The Prayer on the Prophet (p.b.u.h.)

Ahmad related in his **Musnad** and ad-Diya in **al-Mukhtar** from Amir bin Rabi'a with a good **isnad** that the Messenger of Allah (peace and blessings of Allah be upon him) said:

"There is no slave who prays for blessings on me but that the angels pray on him as long as he prays on me. So let the slave do a little or a lot of it."

Visiting the Sick

Ibn-Hibban said in his **Sahih** with sound **isnad** from Ali' (may Allah be pleased with him) that the Messenger of Allah (peace and blessings of Allah be upon him) said:

"No Muslims visits another Muslim without a thousand angels praying for blessings on him whatever hour of the day it is until evening, or whatever hour of night it is until morning."

In a variant of at-Tirmidhi which an-Nawawi mentioned in the *Riyad-us-Salihin*, is that the Prophet said:

"No Muslim visits another Muslim without thousand angels praying blessings on him until the evening, or visits him in the evening without a thousand angels praying blessings on him until morning and he will have fruits of Garden."

At-Tirmidhi said that its *isnad* is good.

Visiting Brothers

Muslim transmitted in his *Sahih* from Abu Hurairah (may Allah be pleased with him) that the Prophet of Allah (peace and blessings of Allah be upon him) said:

"A man visited a brother of his in another town and Allah Almighty assigned an angel to guard him on his way. When he came to him, the angel said:

`Where are you going?'

`I am going to visit a brother of mine in that town', he said.

`Do you have any property with him that you want to check on?' he said.

`No, it is only that I love him for the sake of Allah', he said:

"I am the messenger of Allah to you to tell you that Allah loves you as you love this for His sake."

Praying For All Brethren

Allah Almighty says:

وَالَّذِينَ جَآءُوْ مِنْ بَعْدِهِمْ يَقُوْلُوْنَ رَبَّنَا اغْفِرْلَنَا وَلِإِخْوَانِنَا الَّذِينَ سَبَقُوْنَا بِالْإِيْمَانِ وَلَا تَجْعَلْ فِيْ قُلُوْبِنَا غِلًّا لِّلَّذِيْنَ امَنُوْا رَبَّنَآ اِنَّكَ رَءُوْفٌ رَّحِيْمٌ

" And those who came after them say: 'Our Lord! forgive us

, and our brethren who came before us into the Faith and leave not, in our hearts, rancour(or sense of injury) against those who have believed. Our Lord! Thou art indeed Full of Kindness, Most Merciful."

(Q 59:10)

Those that came after them: The immediate meaning would refer to later arrivals in Madinah or later accessions to Islam, compared with the early *Muhajirs*. But the general meaning would include all future comers into the House of Islam. They pray, not only for themselves but for all their brethren and above all, they pray, that their hearts may be purified of any desire or tendency to discharge the work or virtues of other Muslims or to feel any jealousy on account of their successes or good time.

A man who may have suffered or been disappointed may have a lurking sense of injury at the back of his mind which may spoil his enjoyment on account of past memory intruding in the midst of felicity. In such cases memory itself is pain. Even sorrow is intensified by memory. The clouds of the past will have dissolved in glorious light, and no past happiness will be comparable with the perfect happiness which will have then been attained. Nor will any sense of envy or shortcoming be possible in that perfect bliss.

Jesus said: "Blessed are the meek, for they shall inherit the earth", Matt.v.5. Here we are told: blessed are the righteous, for they shall inherit the kingdom of heaven. The stress here is on actual practical deeds of righteousness: whether they find their rewards on the earth or not is immaterial, their attention is directed to an infinitely greater reward, the kingdom of heaven. In the sermon on the Mount this is promised to "poor in spirit", Matt.v.3.

Muslim transmitted from the **hadith** of Abu Darda that the

Prophet of Allah(peace and blessings of Allah be upon him) said:

> "A supplication which a Muslim makes secretly for his brother is answered. At his guard is a guardian angel. Whenever he makes supplication for good for his brother, the angel who guard him says, 'Amen' and the same for you."

Sleeping in a State of Wudu

Umar Ibn Khattab(may Allah be pleased with him)said that the messenger of Allah(peace and blessings of Allah be upon him) said:

> "Whoever spends the night in a state of purity, spends the night with an angel close to him. He does not wake up without the angel saying:

> "O Allah, forgive Your slave so-and-so, He has, spent the night in a state of purity."

Ibn Hibban related it in his Sahih and al-Mundhiri mentioned it in **at-Targhib Wat-Targhib.**

'Close to him" means what is next to a person's body, be it a garment or anything else.

His words, "He spent the night in a state of purity" is a reason for forgiveness being asked for him. It is part of what the angel said.

Ibn 'Abbas(may Allah be pleased with him) said that he Messenger of Allah(peace and blessings of Allah be upon him)said:

> "Purify those bodies of yours and Allah will purify you. There is no slave who spends the night in a state of purity but that an angel remains close to him. He does not pass an hour of the night without saying.

'O Allah, forgive Your slave. He spent the night in a state of purity."

At-Tabrani related it in **al-Aswat** and al-Mundhiri said that its *isnad* is good.

Cursing the Transgressors and Wrong-Doers

Allah Almighty says:

كَيْفَ يَهْدِى اللَّهُ قَوْمًا كَفَرُوا بَعْدَ إِيمَانِهِمْ وَشَهِدُوا أَنَّ الرَّسُولَ حَقٌّ وَجَاءَهُمُ الْبَيِّنَاتُ وَاللَّهُ لَا يَهْدِى الْقَوْمَ الظَّالِمِينَ ۞ أُولَٰئِكَ جَزَاؤُهُمْ أَنَّ عَلَيْهِمْ لَعْنَةَ اللَّهِ وَالْمَلَائِكَةِ وَالنَّاسِ أَجْمَعِينَ ۞ خَالِدِينَ فِيهَا لَا يُخَفَّفُ عَنْهُمُ الْعَذَابُ وَلَا هُمْ يُنظَرُونَ

"How shall Allah guide those who reject Faith after they accepted and bore witness that the Messenger was true and that Clear Signs had come unto them? But Allah guides not a people unjust. Of such the reward is that on them (rests) the curse of Allah and His Angels and of all mankind; In that will they dwell; nor will their punishment be lightened, nor respite be their (lot)
(Q. 3:86-88).

Allah Almighty says:

إِنَّ الَّذِينَ يَكْتُمُونَ مَا أَنزَلْنَا مِنَ الْبَيِّنَاتِ وَالْهُدَىٰ مِنْ بَعْدِ مَا بَيَّنَّاهُ لِلنَّاسِ فِي الْكِتَابِ أُولَٰئِكَ يَلْعَنُهُمُ اللَّهُ وَيَلْعَنُهُمُ اللَّاعِنُونَ ۞ إِلَّا الَّذِينَ تَابُوا وَأَصْلَحُوا وَبَيَّنُوا فَأُولَٰئِكَ أَتُوبُ عَلَيْهِمْ وَأَنَا التَّوَّابُ الرَّحِيمُ ۞ إِنَّ الَّذِينَ كَفَرُوا وَمَاتُوا وَهُمْ كُفَّارٌ أُولَٰئِكَ عَلَيْهِمْ لَعْنَةُ اللَّهِ وَالْمَلَائِكَةِ وَالنَّاسِ أَجْمَعِينَ ۞

خَالِدِينَ فِيهَا لَا يُخَفَّفُ عَنْهُمُ الْعَذَابُ
وَلَاهُمْ يُنظَرُونَ

"Those who conceal the clear (Signs) We have sent down, and the Guidance, after We have made it clear for the people in the Book;---on them shall be Allah's curse, and the curse of those entitled to curse. Except those who repent and make amends and openly declare (the Truth) : to them I turn; for I am oft-Returning, Most Merciful. Those who reject Faith and die rejecting, on them is Allah's curse and the curse of angels, and of all mankind. They will abide therein: their penalty will not be lightened nor will respite be their (lot)
(Q. 2:159-162).

Those entitled to curse i.e. angels and mankind: the cursed one will deprive themselves of the protection of Allah and of the angels, and of the good wishes of mankind, because by contimaciously rejecting Faith, they not only sin against Allah but are false to their own manhood, which Allah created in the "**best of moulds**". The terrible curses denounced in the Old Testament are set out in Deut. 15-68. There is one difference. Here it is for the deliberate rejection of Faith, a theological term for the denying of our higher nature. There it is for a breach of the least part of the ceremonial Law.

A curse is not a matter of words; it is a terrible state, opposite to the state of Grace. Can man curse? Not of course in the same sense in which we speak of the curse of Allah. A mere verbal curse is of the effect. But if men are opposed or unjustly treated, their cries can ascend to Allah in prayer, and then it becomes Allah's "wrath" or curse, the deprivation of Allah's Grace as regards the wrong-doer.

'By the clear signs and guidance' may mean the general

religous teachings which the Jews tried to conceal, but in the
present context these clear science and guidance have a painted
reference to those clear indications contained in the Torah, by
which the advent of the Last Prophet Muhammad (peace and
blessings of Allah be upon him) could be clearly visualised. The
Jews, instead of making a proper use of these indications, tried to
supress them. One great mischief of the Jews in regard to concealment which has an implied reference in the above-quoted verses is
that they distorted the great fact about al-marwa being the right
place where Hadrat Ibrahim (peace be uponhim)tried to offer
Hadrat Isma'il (peace be upon him) as a sacrifice to the Lord.
Maulana Farahi has brought to light the distortions made by the
Jews in concealing al-Marwa as the place of sacrifice of Hadrat
Isma'il from the Torah. The idea behind it was to suppress the
predictions found in the Torah in regard to the advent of Muhammad
(peace and blessings of Allah be upon him).

Allah's curse means to turn away from His Grace. In classical
Arabic usages, the word *la'nah* is equivalent to *ih'ad* (estrange-
ment or banishment).

All righteous persons who are competent to judge moral
issues are referred to here. The other is that it includes all animate
and inanimate beings, who are hit because of the calamities falling
upon the earth due to the mischiefs of the mischief-mongers.

The repentence is effective only when it is accompanied by
a strong determination to make amends for the wrong done in the
past and to improve one's behaviour in future.

Allah Almighty says:

اِنَّ الَّذِيْنَ كَفَرُوْا وَمَاتُوْا وَهُمْ كُفَّارٌ اُولٰٓئِكَ عَلَيْهِمْ لَعْنَةُ اللهِ وَالْمَلٰٓئِكَةِ
وَالنَّاسِ اَجْمَعِيْنَ

"Verily those who disbelieve and die while they are disbelievers, these are on whom shall be the curse of Allah, and(that of) the angels, and of men all together" (Q. 2:161).

In the above *ayah* are mentioned those who obstinately adhered to the path of disbelief and made no effort to change their attitude of the denial of the Truth, and of concealing the Truth. The word *ajma'in* (all) alongwith *an'nas* is meant to show that on the day of Resurrection, when the Truth would be made manifest before the whole mankind, not only the pious and virtuous, who have genuine right to curse disbelievers and concealers of Truth would curse them but even those sinners would hurl curses upon them who were misled by them in this mortal world.

According to another scholar **ajma'in** is not coupled with **an'nas** but it is meant to indicate that Allah, angels, and the righteous people all combined together would curse the disbelievers.

Curse on those Preventing the Implementation of Divine Code

In the **Sunan** of an-Nasa'i, Abu Dawud and Ibn Majah with sound **isnad** from ibn 'Abbas (may Allah be pleased with him) and his father, is that the Messenger of Allah (peace and blessings of Allah be upon him) said:

"If anyone is murdered deliberately, someone should be killed in retaliation. Taking place on him is the curse of Allah, the angels and all people."

Thus there is a curse on anyone who prevents the implementation of the judgement of Allah on someone who has murdered deliberately for the sake of rank or wealth. So how much more must this be the case when someone tries to prevent the implementation of the **Shari'ah** as a whole!

Cursing Innovators

Among those Allah and His angels curse are who innovate in the **deen** of Allah by abandoning its judgements and transgressig against its laws or sheltering and protecting people who do that, as has come in the sound **hadith**:

> "Anyone who makes an innovation or shelters those who make innovations, on him is the curse of Allah, the angels and all people."

Abu Dawud, an-Nasa'i and al-Hakam transmitted it.

Cursing those Abusing the Companions of the Messengers of Allah

In the collection of at-Tibrani, **al kabir**, Abbas (may Allah be pleased with him) said that the Prophet of Allah (peace and blessings of Allah be upon him) said:

> "Anyone who abuses my Companion, on him is the curse of Allah, the angels and all people."

Women Disobeying their Husbands

Al-Bukhari transmitted with his **isnad** from Abu Hurairah (may Allah be pleased with him) that the Prophet of Allah (peace and blessings of Allah be upon him) said:

> "When a woman spends the night spurning her husband's bed, the angels curse her until she returns."

In another variant:

"When a man calls his wife to bed and she refuses to come, the angels curse her until morning."

In a third variant in the **Sahih** of al-Bukhari:

"When a man calls his wife to bed and she does not come and he spends the night angry with her, the angels curse her until morning."

Ibn Hajr said in **al-Fath**:

"About the words of Prophet of Allah (peace and blessings of Allah be upon him) `She refuses to come', Abu `Awana adds in a variant, `and he spends the night angry with her.' It is through this addition that 'he curse occurs because it is by that her rebellion is confirmed' which is not the case when he is not angry about it. It might be that he excuses her or that he abandons his right. Censure is only directed against her when she is the one who spurns him and he is angry about it, or he spurns her because she is wrong-doing and does not renounce her wrong action. If he is the one who begins wrongly to spurn her, then it is another case."

He also said, "This *hadith* carries in it permission to curse a Muslim who is disobeying Allah if it is done in order to alarm him so that he will not engage in it, then you should ask for repentance and guidance for him. It shows that the angels continue cursing the people of disobedience as long as they are doing it.

"It guides women to helping their husbands and seeking to please them and it shows that men are less patient with regard to lack of sex than women, disclosing that the strongest cause of disturbance for a man is his impulse for lawful sexual intercourse. That is why the Law giver makes it mand-atory for women to help men in respect of it.

It also goes to show that continuing to obey Allah and being steadfast in worshpping Him is in itself a reward for His slave since Allah did not omit any of his rights or fail to have them taken care of, to the extent that he has even made the angels curse someone who angers His slave by denying one of his appetites. In the same way it is therefore obligatory for the slave to fulfil the rights his Lord has over him."

Woman Going Out Without Her Husband's Permission

Ibn `Umar (may Allah be pleased with him) said:

"I saw a woman who came to the Prophet of Allah (peace and blessings of Allah be upon him), and said:

"Messenger of Allah, what right does a husband have over his wife?' He said, `His right over her is that she does not leave his house without his permission. If she does that, the angels of mercy and angels of anger curse her until she repents or returns."

The *hadith* is related by Abu Dawud, at-Tabalisi and al-Bazzar.

On Pointing at One's Brother With a Weapon

Muslim related in his **Sahih** that Abu Hurairah (may Allah be pleased with him) said that the Prophet of Allah (peace and blessings of Allah be upon him) said:

"If someone points with a piece of iron at his brother, the angels curse him until he puts it down, even if it is his full brother."

Scholars say that the words of the Prophet of Allah (peace and blessings of Allah be upon him) "the angels curse him" is to emphasise the general prohibition against anyone whether he is hostile or not, whether in just a threat or in earnest, because to alarm a Muslim is absolutely unlawful. The curse of the angel on anyone who does it shows how unlawful it is.

Ibn al-Arabi said:

"If someone who merely points with a weapon deserves the curse, then what about someone who actually strikes with one? The pointer merits the curse, as has already been stated, whether his pointing is just as a threat or whether it is in earnest or in jest. Even a joker is punished when he causes fear in his brother, and it is clear that wrong action of a joker is less than that of someone who is serious."

The curse of the angels demonstrates the unlawfulness of this action which makes his brother alarmed and through which Satan might provoke him to kill his brother. This is particularly the case when the weapon concerned is one of these modern ones which can be discharged by the least error on unintentional touch. How many examples of this there are.

On Respecting Angels

The angels are slaves of Allah whom He has selected and chosen and they have a high position with their Lord. The believer who worships Allah and seeks His pleasure must undertake to love and respect the angels and to avoid anything that might vex or harm them.

The things that distress them most are wrong actions, acts of disobedience, disbelief and associating others with Allah. Conversely what pleases the angels most is for a man's *deen* to be sincerely for his Lord and avoidance of all that angers Him."

That is why the angels do not enter places or houses in which Allah Almighty is disobeyed, for those in which there is something that Allah dislikes and hates such as idols, images, and statues. Nor do they go near anyone who is involved in acts of disobedience to Allah such as drunkenness.

Abu Hamid al-Ghazzali said in his **Ihya'** that Abu Hurairah (may Allah be pleased with him) said, "The house in which the Qur'an is recited is spacious for the people in it and its good is abundant and the angels are present in it and the Satans leave it. The house in which the Book of Allah, the Mighty and Exalted, is not recited is narrow for the people in it and has little good and the angels leave it and the Satans are present in it."

Al-Bukhari transmitted with his *isnad* from 'Ubayadullah bin 'Abdullah who heard Ibn' Abbas (may Allah be pleased with him) say:

"I heard Abu Talha say, 'I heard the Messenger of Allah (peace and blessings of Allah be upon him) say;'"

'The angels do not enter house in which there is a dog or an image."

Al-Bazzar related on sound *isnad* from Burayda (may Allah be pleased with him) that the Messenger of Allah (peace and blessings of Allah be upon him), said:

"There are three whom the angels do not go near: Someone who is drunk, someone wearing Saffron, and someone in *janaba*."

The angels are harmed by the same things that harm the sons

of Adam, and this is confirmed in sound **hadiths**. They are harmed by foul smells, filth and dirt.

Al-Bukhari and Muslim related that the Messenger of Allah (peace and blessings of Allah be upon him) said:

> "Anyone who eats garlic and onions or leeks should not come near our Mosque. The angels are harmed by what harms the sons of Adam."

Ibn Khuzayma and Ibn Hibban transmitted that Abu Ayyub said that the Messenger of Allah (peace and blessings Allah be upon him), was sent some food which consisted of vegetables and which contained onions or leeks. He did not see the Messenger of Allah (peace and blessings of Allah be upon him) choose it, so he refused to eat as well. He said to him, "What is stopping you?" He said, "I did not see the trace of your hand." He said, "I am shy before the angels of Allah. It is not forbidden."

In one variant we find: "Eat, I speak intimately with those with whom you did not speak intimately", i.e. the angels.

Spitting to the right during the prayer

The messenger of Allah (peace and blessings of Allah be upon him) forbade spitting to the right during the prayer because when a person stands in prayer, the angel stands on his right. In the **Sahih** of Al-Bukhari from Abu Hurairah (may Allah be pleased with him) is that the Prophet (peace and blessings of Allah be upon him) said:

> "When one of you stands for the prayer, he should not spit in front of him for he is speaking with Allah as long as he is in his prayer, nor to his right, for there is an angel on his right. He should spit to his left or under his foot and bury it."

In general, all believers should be God-conscious, and clean. The bearers of the Throne(i.e. Angels) start chanting "Glory be to Allah!" "Glory be to Allah!" out of terror and this stream of terror goes down to the angels in the lowest heaven and they all start glorifying Allah, the Exalted. When the terror of their hearts subsides to a great extent, the Angels below the Angels bearing the Throne ask them about the new order of the Almighty and the news goes down to the Angels in the lowest heaven."

From the holy Qur'an and the **hadith** it is manifest that the Angels are separate creation, have speech faculty, walk on earth, fear Allah Almighty and keep on glorifying Him. Allah Almighty runs His administration of the universe through these Angels. Hence they are called a link between Allah and the universe.

Besides the above functions they have fought against the Unbelievers being armed with the required weapons and revelation came to the last Prophet (peace and blessings of Allah be upon him) with the *ayahs* of the holy Qur'an. They keep glorifying Allah Almighty and obeying Him by encircling His Throne. They also come into contact and speak to men of Heaven and Hell.

Angels have also been deputed by Allah Almighty to guard men in calamities. The holy Qur'an says:

$$لَهُ مُعَقِّبَاتٌ مِّنْ بَيْنِ يَدَيْهِ وَمِنْ خَلْفِهِ يَحْفَظُونَهُ$$
$$مِنْ أَمْرِ اللّٰهِ ۗ$$

For each (such person) there are (angels) in succession, before and behind him: they guard him by command of Allah."   (Q. 13:11).

That is, every person whether he conceals or reveals his brothers, whether he sulks in darkness or goes about by day, all are under Allah's watch and ward. His grace encompasses everyone, and again and again protects him, if he will only take the protection, from harm and evil, or in his folly he thinks he can secretly take some pleasure or profit, he is wrong, for recording angels record all his thoughts and deeds.

There are angels who write down Records of men. The Holy Qur'an says:

$$ وَإِنَّ عَلَيْكُمْ لَحَفِظِينَ ۞ كِرَامًا كَاتِبِينَ ۞ يَعْلَمُونَ مَا تَفْعَلُونَ $$

"But verily over you (are appointed angels) to protect you, kind and honourable, -- writing down (your deeds): They know all that ye do." (Q. 82:10-12).

Besides the faculties given to man to guide him, and the form and personality through which he can rise by stages to the presence of Allah, there are spiritual agencies around him, and to note down his Record, so that perfect justice may be done to him at the end. The Holy Qur'an says in Surah Qaf:

$$ إِذْ يَتَلَقَّى الْمُتَلَقِّيَانِ عَنِ الْيَمِينِ وَعَنِ الشِّمَالِ قَعِيدٌ ۞ مَا يَلْفِظُ مِنْ $$
$$ قَوْلٍ إِلَّا لَدَيْهِ رَقِيبٌ عَتِيدٌ ۞ $$

"Behold, two (guardian angels) appointed to learn (his doings), learn (and note them), one sitting on the right and one on the left. Not a word does he utter but there is a vigilant Guardian. (Q.50:17-18)

Two angels are constantly by him to note his thoughts, words and actions. One sits on the right side and notes his good deeds and the other on the left, to note his bad deeds; corresponding to the Companions of the Right and Companions of the Left mentioned. Then each "Word" spoken is taken down by a guardian. This has been constred to mean that the guardian only records words, not thought to which are not uttered. Thoughts may be forgiven if not uttered, and still more if they do not issue in action. At the stage at which we clothe a thought in words, we have already done an action. The Records mentioned in the last verse make a complete Record, in order to supply motives and springs of action, which will affect the degrees or status in the Hereafter.

About their administrative functions the holy Qur'an says:

وَالذَّارِيَاتِ ذَرْوًا ۞ فَالْحَامِلَاتِ وِقْرًا ۞ فَالْجَارِيَاتِ يُسْرًا ۞ فَالْمُقَسِّمَاتِ أَمْرًا

"By the (Winds) that scatter broadcast; and those that lift and bear away heavy weights; and those that flow with ease and gentleness and those that distribute. (Q. 51: 1-4).

Four things are mentioned in *ayah* 1 to 4 as evidences or types of the certainty and unity of a Truth described in *ayah* 5-6:

إِنَّمَا تُوعَدُونَ لَصَادِقٌ ۞ وَإِنَّ الدِّينَ لَوَاقِعٌ ۞

"verily that which ye are promised is true; and verily judgement and justice will surely come to pass."

What these things are is described by certain adjectival participles, the noun understood being usually taken to be "Winds": the word for Wind *(Rih)* being feminine in Arabic. Some commentators however understand other nouns as being implied. e.g., angels in all four verses, or different things in each of the four verses. Whatever these things are, their different modes of working are evidence of the power and goodness of Allah, the Unity of His Plan, and the certainty of Good and Evil reaching their own destined ends, when judgement and Justice will have given each one his due.

Winds may blow strong, and scatter particles of dust far and wide; but they do not diminish by one jot the substance of Allah's material creation; on the contrary help to readjust things. They reshape the configuration of the earth in the vegetable kingdom. They carry seeds about and plant new seeds in old soils; in the

region of air they produce mighty changes in temperature and
pressure that effect animal and vegetable life; they carry the
moisture of equatorial Africa to the parched plains of India and so
on. Yet they are just one little agency showing Allah's working with
amterial world. So in the spiritual world Revelation works mighty
changes; it may be resisted, but the resistance will be swept away;
it ever points to the one Great Final Event, "to which the whole
Creation moves."

The things that lift and bear away heavy weights may be the
winds that carry the heavey rain-clouds or that sweep off every
resistance from their path, or it may be the heavy moisture-laden
clouds themselves. So works Revelation: it lifts and sweeps away
the burdens of custom, superstition, or man's inertia, and ever leads
onwards to the destined End.

These may be Winds that fill the sails of ships with gentle and
favourable breezes, that carry men and merchandise to their
destinations. Or they may be the ships themselves, whose smooth
motion through the water is described in many places, by the verb
Jara, "to flow", e.g. *surah 2 ayah 164* :

إِنَّ فِى خَلْقِ السَّمٰوٰتِ وَالْأَرْضِ وَاخْتِلَافِ الَّيْلِ
وَالنَّهَارِ وَالْفُلْكِ الَّتِى تَجْرِى فِى الْبَحْرِ بِمَا يَنْفَعُ النَّاسَ وَمَاأَنْزَلَ
اللهُ مِنَ السَّمَآءِ مِنْ مَّآءٍ فَأَحْيَا بِهِ الْأَرْضَ بَعْدَ مَوْتِهَا
وَبَثَّ فِيهَا مِنْ كُلِّ دَآبَّةٍ وَّتَصْرِيفِ الرِّيٰحِ وَالسَّحَابِ
الْمُسَخَّرِ بَيْنَ السَّمَآءِ وَالْأَرْضِ لَأٰيٰتٍ لِّقَوْمٍ يَّعْقِلُونَ

"Behold! In the creation of the heavens and the earth; in the
alternation of the Night and Day; in the sailing of the ships
through the Ocean for the profit of mankind in the rain which
Allah sends donw from the skies, and the life which He gives
therewith to an earth that is dead; in the beasts of all kinds

that He scatters through the earth in the change of the winds
and the clouds which they trail like their slaves between the
sky and the earth; --- (here) indeed are Sings for a people
that are wise."   (Q. 2:164)

These may be Winds (or other agencies) that distribute and
apportion moisture or rain or atmosphere pressure or other
blessings of Allah, not haphazard but by fixed laws, i.e., according
to the Command of their Lord. So with Revelation. Its blessings are
distributed all round, and it produces its marvellous effects sometimes in the most unlikely places and ways.

These angels keep glorifying Allah Almighty without feeling
any fatigue and exhaustion. The Holy Qur'an says:

فَإِنِ اسْتَكْبَرُوا فَالَّذِينَ عِندَ رَبِّكَ يُسَبِّحُونَ لَهُ

بِالَّيْلِ وَالنَّهَارِ وَهُمْ لَا يَسْأَمُونَ

"But if the (Unbelievers) are arrogant (no matter): for in the
presence of thy Lord are those who celebrate His praises by
night and by day. And they never flag (nor feel themselves
about it).   (Q. 41:38)

It does not in any way affect Allah if men rebel agianst Him.
It is men's own loss. Allah is being celebrated night and day by
angels or men who receive the privilege of approaching His
presence. To them it is delight and an honour to be in the sunshine
of Truth and happiness.

These angels help the Believers and Friends of Allah in armed
struggle against the enemies of Allah Almighty, as they have done
in the Battle of Badr. The holy Qur'an says:

إِذْ تَسْتَغِيثُونَ رَبَّكُمْ فَاسْتَجَابَ لَكُمْ أَنِّي مُمِدُّكُم بِأَلْفٍ
مِّنَ الْمَلَائِكَةِ مُرْدِفِينَ

"Remember ye implored the assistance of your Lord, and
he answered you: `I will assist you with a thousand of the
angels, ranks on ranks."   (Q. 8:9)

The number of angels, a thousand at Badr and three thousand
and five at Uhad, is equal to the strength of the enemy. The holy
Qur'an says :

وَلَقَدْ نَصَرَكُمُ اللهُ بِبَدْرٍ وَأَنْتُمْ

اَذِلَّةٌ فَاتَّقُوا اللهَ لَعَلَّكُمْ تَشْكُرُونَ ۞ اِذْ تَقُولُ لِلْمُؤْمِنِينَ

اَلَنْ يَكْفِيَكُمْ اَنْ يُمِدَّكُمْ رَبُّكُمْ بِثَلَاثَةِ اَلَافٍ مِنَ الْمَلَائِكَةِ

مُنْزَلِينَ ۞ بَلَى اِنْ تَصْبِرُوا وَتَتَّقُوا وَيَأْتُوكُمْ مِنْ فَوْرِهِمْ

هَذَا يُمْدِدْكُمْ رَبُّكُمْ بِخَمْسَةِ اَلَافٍ مِنَ الْمَلَائِكَةِ مُسَوِّمِينَ

وَمَا جَعَلَهُ اللهُ اِلَّا بُشْرَى لَكُمْ وَلِتَطْمَئِنَّ قُلُوبُكُمْ بِهِ وَمَا

النَّصْرُ اِلَّا مِنْ عِنْدِ اللهِ الْعَزِيزِ الْحَكِيمِ

"Allah had helped you at Badr when ye were helpless; then
fear Allah: thus may ye show your gratitude. Remember thou
saidst to the Faithful: "Is it not enough for you that Allah
should help you with three thousand angels (specially) sent
down?

"Yea, if ye remain firm, and act aright, even if the enemy
should rush here on you in hot haste, your Lord would help
you with five thousand angels clearly marked."

Allah made it but a message of hope for you, and an
assurance to your hearts: (in any case) there is no victory
except from Allah, the Exalted, the Wise." (Q. 3:123-126)

These angels cannot even move an inch without the order and
leave of Allah Almighty. The holy Qur'an says :

وَمَانَتَنَزَّلُ إِلَّا بِأَمْرِ رَبِّكَ لَهُ مَابَيْنَ أَيْدِينَا وَمَاخَلْفَنَا وَمَابَيْنَ ذَلِكَ
وَمَاكَانَ رَبُّكَ نَسِيًّا۞ رَبُّ السَّمْوَتِ وَ الْأَرْضِ وَمَابَيْنَهُمَا فَاعْبُدْهُ
وَاصْطَبِرْ لِعِبَادَتِهِ هَلْ تَعْلَمُ لَهُ سَمِيًّا

"(The angels say:) "We descend not but by command of thy
Lord: to Him belongeth what is before us and what is behind
us, and what is in between: and thy Lord never doth forget
-- Lord of the heavens and of the earth and of all that is
between them: So worship Him, and be constant and patient
in His worship: knowest thou of any who is worthy of the
same Name as He?   (Q. 19:64-65).

We are apt to be impatient of the evils we see around us. We
may give of our best service to Allah, and yet see no results. In our
human short-sightedness we may complain within ourselves. But
we must not be impatient. The angels of Grace come not haphazard, but by command of Allah according to His Universal Will and
Purpose. Allah does not forget. If things are delayed, it is in
accordance with a wise providence, which cares for all. Our plain
duty is to be patient and constant in His service.

The more we taste of the truth and mystery of life, the more
do we realise that there is no one to be mentioned in the same breath
as Allah. He is above all names. But when we think of His beautiful
qualities, and picture them to ourselves by names which give us
some idea of Him, we can search the whole wide world of
imagination and we shall not find another to be compared with Him
in name or quality. He is the One: praise be to Him!

Crores of such angels dot about the universe and their exact
number is known to Allah alone Imam Ghazzali writes in his book
entitled "Kimiya-e-Sa`adat":

"The beginning of all the works of Allah is one of the

attributes of Allah and His Will is derived right from this attribute. And as the will to write anything is reflected first on the heart and goes to other parts only through the heart, in the same way the reflection of the Will of Allah is first cast on the Throne and then goes to others. Allah's Will is carried to all sphere of activities through His angels."

Allah is All-mighty and All-Powerful. What man has in the form of power and control come to him from Divine Attributes. What man has in the form of power is insecure, imperfect and subject to change and transition, while the attributes of Allah are Perfect, Sovereign and beyond the reach of any power whatsoever. However Allah Almighty seeks to complete His power and control through the angels who are the Light of Allah.

The Holy Qur'an says :

$$\text{وَمَا يَعْلَمُ جُنُودَ رَبِّكَ اِلَّا هُوَ}$$

"......and none can know the forces of the Lord, except He"
(Q. 74:31)

It is a necessary consequence of moral responsibility and freedom of choice in man, that he should be left free to stray if he chooses to do so in spite of all the warning and instruction he receives. Allah's channels of warning and instruction -- His spiritual forces --- are infinite, as are His power. No man can know them. But this warning or reminder is addressed to all mankind.

Astonishing balance and harmony among the stars and planets are only due to these angels who run and control and maintain balance in flawless expertness. What to speak of space journey and going to the moon, even a dust particle and a little straw cannot stir without the command of Allah and the administrative perfection of the angels bestowed on them by the Almighty Himself. But they are not visible due to their delicate bodies. The Holy Qur'an says:

لَايَعْزُبُ عَنْهُ مِثْقَالُ ذَرَّةٍ فِى السَّمٰوٰتِ وَلَا فِى الْأَرْضِ وَلَا أَصْغَرُ مِنْ ذٰلِكَ وَلَا أَكْبَرُ إِلَّا فِى كِتٰبٍ مُّبِيْنٍ

"From Whom is not hidden the least little atom in the Heavens or on earth, nor is there anything less than that, or greater, but is in the Record Perspicuous." (Q. 34:3)

In the symbolical language of our own human experience, a record is more enduring than memory: in fact (if properly preserved) it is perpetual. If further it is expressed in clear language, without any obscurity, it can always be read with perfect precision and without any doubt whatever. Apply these qualities, free from human defect to Allah's law and decrees. They are unerring and enduring. Everything, great or small, will receive due recognition - --- a Reward for Good and a punishment for Evil.

The Holy Qur'an says :

صِرَاطِ اللهِ الَّذِى لَهُ مَا فِى السَّمٰوٰتِ وَمَا فِى الْأَرْضِ أَلَا إِلَى اللهِ تَصِيْرُ الْأُمُوْرُ

"The way of Allah, to Whom belongs whatever is in the heavens and whatever is on the earth. Behold (how) all affairs tend towards Allah!" (Q. 42:53)

Shah Waliullah Muhaddith Dehlvi writes in his book *Hujjat-ul-Baligha*:

"A large body of the angels have been entrusted with the task of infusing in the heart of His creation such thought which may lead to some creative work."

He further writes:

"Sometimes two armies are engaged in terrible wars. In such a situation a group of angels descend to encourage and bring about peace and firmness to the hearts of the troops on one side and paving the way to success by extending them practical help in the armed struggle. While another party is discouraged and disheartened to accept defeat."

The following *ayah* of the Qur'an suggests the same :

وَأَنْزَلَ جُنُودًا لَّمْ تَرَوْهَا، وَعَذَّبَ الَّذِيْنَ كَفَرُوْا، وَذٰلِكَ جَزَآءُ الْكٰفِرِيْنَ۞

"And sent down forces which ye saw not: He punished the Unbelievers: thus doth He reward those without Faith."

(Q. 9:26)

The Prophet never approved of over-weening confidence, reliance merely upon human strength, or human resources or numbers. In the hour of danger and seeming disaster, he was perfectly calm, and with cool courage relied upon the help of Allah Whose standard he carried. His calmness inspired all around him, and stopped the rout of those who had turned their backs. It was Allah's help that they won, and their victory was complete. They followed it up with an energetic pursuit of the enemies, capturing their camps, their flocks and herds, and their families, whom they had boastfully brought with them in expectation of an easy victory

Every work of Allah Almighty is performed with a definite programme and on the appointed hours. His purpose is served and programme fulfilled through men and angels. And man's ascending to the moon and his space research is a part of the same system by which Allah Almighty had to introduce His Magnificence, Power and grandeur to men. It is the law of nature to award fruits of man's efforts, patience and firmness.

The Holy Qur'an says :

وَأَنَّ سَعْيَهُ سَوْفَ يُرٰى

"That (the fruit of) his striving will soon come in sight.

(Q. 53:40)

That is, man must strive, or he will gain nothing; and that if he strives, the result must soon appear in sight and we will find his reward in full measure. It is constant striving and struggle which leads to final success. Striving men earn the permission and pleasure of Allah Almighty Who helps such men with His angels. Man's success in Space Research is the result of human strivings for centuries. Having reached in space and planets one comes to experience astonishing sense of the goodness and greatness of Allah Almighty and His magnificient power and grandeur. In this way the authenticity of the Holy Qur'an comes to light beyond an iota of doubt.

The Holy Qur'an says :

لَقَدۡ خَلَقۡنَاالۡإِنۡسَانَ فِیۡ کَبَدٍ

"Verily We have created man into toil and struggle."

(Q. 90:4)

"Man is born into troubles as the sparks fly upward"

(Job, v.7); "For all his days are sorrows, and his travail grief" (Eeclesiastes, ii.23). Man's life is full of sorrow and vexation; but our text has a different shade of meaning: man is born to strive and struggle; and if he suffers from hardships, he must exercise patience, for Allah will make his way smooth for him. On the other hand no man should boast of worldly goods or worldly prosperity.